Melissa O. Hawkins, MS
Francis A. McGuire, PhD
Kenneth F. Backman, PhD
Editors

Preparing Participants for Intergenerational Interaction: Training for Success

Preparing Participants for Intergenerational Interaction: Training for Success has been co-published simultaneously as *Activities, Adaptation & Aging*, Volume 23, Numbers 1, 2, and 3 1999.

*Pre-publication
REVIEWS,
COMMENTARIES,
EVALUATIONS . . .*

"**A** very practical, hands-on approach to training volunteers. . . . The exercises, handouts, and transparencies should be very useful to persons designing and implementing intergenerational training programs."

M. Jean Keller, EdD, CTRS
*Dean, College of Education
Professor of Recreation
and Leisure Studies
University of North Texas*

"**A**ny agency or organization that has given consideration to initiating intergenerational programming would be well-served in reading and implementing the useful training methods presented in *Preparing Participants for Intergenerational Interaction: Training for Success*, edited by Hawkins, Backman, and McGuire. The emphasis here is clearly on training as the authors have effectively taken conceptual and real-world information and packaged it in a way that staff could begin training for intergenerational activities with a minimum amount of time. Chapters are well-conceived with excellent training exercises, ready-to-use transparencies, and current resources including those via the internet.

In this reviewer's opinion, the authors have succeeded in presenting a user-friendly training regimen appropriate to those beginning or seeking to improve intergenerational programs."

Ted Tedrick
Professor
Sport Management
and Leisure Studies
Temple University

The Haworth Press, Inc.

Preparing Participants
for
Intergenerational Interaction:
Training for Success

Preparing Participants for Intergenerational Interaction: Training for Success has been co-published simultaneously as *Activities, Adaptation & Aging*, Volume 23, Numbers 1, 2 and 3 1999.

The *Activities, Adaptation & Aging* Monographs/"Separates"

Drama Activities with Older Adults, by Anne H. Thurman and Carol Ann Piggins

Activities and the "Well Elderly," edited by Phyllis Foster

Pets and the Elderly: The Therapeutic Bond, by Odean Cusack and Elaine Smith

Expressive Therapy with Elders and the Disabled: Touching the Heart of Life, by Jules C. Weiss

Educational Activity Programs for Older Adults: A 12-Month Idea Guide for Adult Education Instructors and Activity Directors in Gerontology, by Janice Lake Williams and Janet Downs

Writers Have No Age: Creative Writing with Older Adults, by Lenore M. Coberly, Jeri McCormick, and Karen Updike

Innovations in Activities for the Elderly: Proceedings of the National Association of Activity Professionals Convention, edited by Jane D. Cook

What Do I Do? How to Care for, Comfort, and Commune with Your Nursing Home Elder, by Katherine L. Karr

Leisure in Later Life: A Sourcebook for the Provision of Recreational Services for Elders, by Michael J. Leitner and Sara F. Leitner

Computer Technology and the Aged: Implications and Applications for Activity Programs, edited by Francis A. McGuire

Therapeutic Activities with the Impaired Elderly, edited by Phyllis M. Foster

Handbook of Group Activities for Impaired Adults, by Elsbeth Martindale and Scott Cabot Willis

Waiting at the Gate: Creativity and Hope in the Nursing Home, by Susan Sandel and David Read Johnson

"You Bring Out the Music in Me": Music in Nursing Homes, edited by Beckie Karras

The Human Factor in Nursing Home Care, by David B. Oliver and Sally Tureman

Adult Day Care: A Practical Guidebook and Manual, by Lenore A. Tate and Cynthia M. Brennan

Geragogy: A Theory for Teaching the Elderly, by Martha Tyler John

The "Feeling Great!" Wellness Program for Older Adults, by Jules C. Weiss

From Deep Within: Poetry Workshops in Nursing Homes, edited by Carol F. Peck

Creative Arts with Older People, by Janice McMurray

Activities with Developmentally Disabled Elderly and Older Adults, edited by M. Jean Keller

Activities in Action: Proceedings of the National Association of Activity Professionals 1990 Conference, edited by Phyllis M. Foster

Story Writing in a Nursing Home: A Patchwork of Memories, edited by Martha Tyler John

Therapeutic Humor with the Elderly, by Francis A. McGuire, Rosangela K. Boyd, and Ann James

Ethics and Values in Long Term Health Care, edited by Patricia J. Villani

Aging Families and Use of Proverbs for Values Enrichment, edited by Vera R. Jackson

Volunteerism in Geriatric Settings, edited by Vera R. Jackson

Exercise Programming for Older Adults, edited by Janie Clark

The Abusive Elder: Service Considerations, edited by Vera R. Jackson

Older Adults with Developmental Disabilities and Leisure: Issues, Policy, and Practice, edited by Ted Tedrick

Horticultural Therapy and the Older Adult Population, edited by Suzanne E. Wells

Preparing Participants for Intergenerational Interaction: Training for Success, edited by Melissa O. Hawkins, Francis A. McGuire, and Kenneth F. Backman

These books were published simultaneously as special thematic issues of *Activities, Adaptation & Aging* and are available bound separately. Visit Haworth's website at http://www.haworthpressinc.com to search our online catalog for complete tables of contents and ordering information for these and other publications. Or call 1-800-HAWORTH (outside US/Canada: 607-722-5857), Fax: 1-800-895-0582 (outside US/Canada: 607-771-0012), or e-mail getinfo@haworthpressinc.com

Preparing Participants for Intergenerational Interaction: Training for Success has also been published as *Activities, Adaptation & Aging*™, Volume 23, Numbers 1, 2 and 3, 1999.

The development, preparation, and publication of this work has been undertaken with great care. However, the publisher, employees, editors, and agents of The Haworth Press and all imprints of The Haworth Press, Inc., including The Haworth Medical Press® and Pharmaceutical Products Press®, are not responsible for any errors contained herein or for consequences that may ensue from use of materials or information contained in this work. Opinions expressed by the author(s) are not necessarily those of The Haworth Press, Inc.

Cover design by Thomas J. Mayshock Jr.

Library of Congress Cataloging-in-Publication Data

Preparing participants for intergenerational interaction : training for success / Melissa O. Hawkins, Francis A. McGuire, Kenneth F. Backman, editors.
     p. cm.
     Has been co-published simultaneously as Activities, adaptation & aging, vol. 23, no.1, 2, and 3 1999.
     Includes bibliographical references and index.
     ISBN 0-7890-0367-8 (alk. paper).
     1. Mentoring–United States 2. Group relations training–United States. 3. Intergenerational relations–Study and teaching–United States. 4. Multicultural education–United States. I. Hawkins, Melissa O. II. McGuire, Francis A. III. Backman, Kenneth F. IV. Activities, adaptation, & aging
HM134 .P74 1998   98-31395
302'.14–dc21   CIP

Preparing Participants
for
Intergenerational Interaction:
Training for Success

Melissa O. Hawkins, MS
Francis A. McGuire, PhD
Kenneth F. Backman, PhD
Editors

Preparing Participants for Intergenerational Interaction: Training for Success has been co-published simultaneously as *Activities, Adaptation & Aging*, Volume 23, Numbers 1, 2 and 3 1999.

The Haworth Press, Inc.
New York • London

INDEXING & ABSTRACTING

Contributions to this publication are selectively indexed or abstracted in print, electronic, online, or CD-ROM version(s) of the reference tools and information services listed below. This list is current as of the copyright date of this publication. See the end of this section for additional notes.

- *Abstracts in Social Gerontology: Current Literature on Aging,* National Council on the Aging, Library, 409 Third Street SW, 2nd Floor, Washington, DC 20024

- *Abstracts of Research in Pastoral Care & Counseling,* Loyola College, 7135 Minstrel Way, Suite 101, Columbia, MD 21045

- *AgeInfo CD-ROM,* Centre for Policy on Ageing, 25-31 Ironmonger Row, London EC1V 3QP, England

- *AgeLine Database,* American Association of Retired Persons, 601 E Street, NW, Washington, DC 20049

- *Alzheimer's Disease Education & Referral Center (ADEAR),* Combined Health Information Database (CHID), P.O. Box 8250, Silver Spring, MD 20907-8250

- *Brown University Geriatric Research Application Digest "Abstracts Section,"* Brown University, Center for Gerontology & Health Care Research, c/o Box G-B 235, Providence, RI 02912

- *Cambridge Scientific Abstracts, Risk Abstracts,* 7200 Wisconsin Avenue #601, Bethesda, MD 20814

- *CINAHL (Cumulative Index to Nursing & Allied Health Literature), in print, also on CD-ROM from CD PLUS, EBSCO, and SilverPlatter, and online from CDP Online (formerly BRS), Data-Star, and PaperChase. (Support materials include Subject Heading List, Database Search Guide, and instructional video).* CINAHL Information Systems, P. O. Box 871/1509 Wilson Terrace, Glendale, CA 91209-0871

(continued)

- *CNPIEC Reference Guide: Chinese National Directory of Foreign Periodicals,* P.O. Box 88, Beijing, Peoples Republic of China

- *Combined Health Information Database (CHID),* National Institutes of Health, 3 Information Way, Bethesda, MD 20892-3580

- *Communication Abstracts,* Temple University, Communication Sciences Department, Weiss Hall, Philadelphia, PA 19122

- *Family Studies Database (online and CD/ROM),* National Information Services Corporation, 306 East Baltimore Pike, 2nd Floor, Media, PA 19063

- *Health Care Literature Information Network/HECLINET,* Technische Universitat Berlin/Dokumentation Krankenhauswesen, Sekr. A42, Strasse des 17. Juni 135, D 10623 Berlin, Germany

- *Human Resources Abstracts (HRA),* Sage Publications, Inc., 2455 Teller Road, Newbury Park, CA 91320

  IBZ International Bibliography of Periodical Literature, Zeller Verlag GmbH & Co., P.O.B. 1949, d-49009 Osnabruck, Germany

- *INTERNET ACCESS (& additional networks) Bulletin Board for Libraries ("BUBL"), coverage of information resources on INTERNET, JANET, and other networks.*
  - <URL:http://bubl.ac.uk/>
  - The new locations will be found under <URL:http://bubl.ac. uk/link/>.
  - Any existing BUBL users who have problems finding information on the new service should contact the BUBL help line by sending e-mail to <bubl@bubl.ac.uk>.
  The Andersonian Library, Curran Building, 101 St. James Road, Glasgow G4 0NS, Scotland

- *Leisure, Recreation and Tourism Abstracts, c/o CAB International/CAB ACCESS . . . available in print, diskettes updated weekly, and on INTERNET. Providing full bibliographic listings, author affiliation, augmented keyword searching,* CAB International, P.O. Box 100, Wallingford Oxon OX10 8DE, United Kingdom

(continued)

- *Mental Health Abstracts (online through DIALOG),* IFI/Plenum Data Company, 3202 Kirkwood Highway, Wilmington, DE 19808

- *National Clearinghouse for Primary Care Information (NCPCI),* 2070 Chain Bridge Road, Suite 450, Vienna, VA 22182-2536

- *REHABDATA, National Rehabilitation Information Center. Searches are Available in large-print, cassette or Braille format and all are available on PC-compatible diskette. Also accessible via the Internet at http//www.naric.com/naric.* (NARIC), 8455 Colesville Road, Suite 935, Silver Spring, MD 20910-3319

- *New Literature on Old Age,* Centre for Policy on Ageing, 25-31 Ironmonger Row, London EC1V 3QP, England

- *OT BibSys,* American Occupational Therapy Foundation, P. O. Box 31220, Rockville, MD 20824-1220

- *Psychological Abstracts (PsycINFO),* American Psychological Association, P. O. Box 91600, Washington, DC 20090-1600

- *Referativnyi Zhurnal (Abstracts Journal of the All-Russian Institute of Scientific and Technical Information),* 20 Usievich Street, Moscow 125219, Russia

- *Social Planning/Policy & Development Abstracts (SOPODA),* Sociological Abstracts, Inc., P. O. Box 22206, San Diego, CA 92192-0206

- *Social Work Abstracts,* National Association of Social Workers, 750 First Street NW, 8th Floor, Washington, DC 20002

- *Sociological Abstracts (SA),* Sociological Abstracts, Inc., P. O. Box 22206, San Diego, CA 92192-0206

- *Special Educational Needs Abstracts,* Carfax Information Systems, P. O. Box 25, Abingdon, Oxfordshire OX14 3UE, United Kingdom

- *Sport Search,* Sport Information Resource Center, 1600 James Naismith Drive, Suite 107, Gloucester, Ontario K1B 5N4, Canada

(continued)

SPECIAL BIBLIOGRAPHIC NOTES

related to special journal issues (separates)
and indexing/abstracting

☐ indexing/abstracting services in this list will also cover material in any "separate" that is co-published simultaneously with Haworth's special thematic journal issue or DocuSerial. Indexing/abstracting usually covers material at the article/chapter level.

☐ monographic co-editions are intended for either non-subscribers or libraries which intend to purchase a second copy for their circulating collections.

☐ monographic co-editions are reported to all jobbers/wholesalers/approval plans. The source journal is listed as the "series" to assist the prevention of duplicate purchasing in the same manner utilized for books-in-series.

☐ to facilitate user/access services all indexing/abstracting services are encouraged to utilize the co-indexing entry note indicated at the bottom of the first page of each article/chapter/contribution.

☐ this is intended to assist a library user of any reference tool (whether print, electronic, online, or CD-ROM) to locate the monographic version if the library has purchased this version but not a subscription to the source journal.

☐ individual articles/chapters in any Haworth publication are also available through the Haworth Document Delivery Service (HDDS).

Preparing Participants for Intergenerational Interaction: Training for Success

CONTENTS

ABOUT THE EDITORS

Melissa O. Hawkins, MS, is Research Associate in the Retirement and Intergenerational Studies Laboratory at the Strom Thurmond Institute at Clemson University in Clemson, South Carolina. In this capacity, she directs grant projects that focus on issues such as volunteerism and community attachment among older adults and assesses the social, economic, and political impacts of older adults across the state. In 1995, Ms. Hawkins was the Co-Planner for an Intergenerational Institute held at the National Recreation and Park Association annual meeting and co-sponsored by the Strom Thurmond Institute and Clemson University's Department of Parks, Recreation, and Tourism Management. She has published in *Rural Special Education Quarterly, Quarterly Newsletter of the Older Adult Education Network, Journal of Physical Education, Recreation & Dance,* and *Therapeutic Recreation Journal.* She has made several presentations based on her work in projects with older adults and youth and is a member of the Southern Gerontological Society, the American Society on Aging, the National Council on the Aging, the Gerontological Society of America, and the National Recreation and Park Association.

Francis A. McGuire, PhD, is Professor in the Department of Parks, Recreation, and Tourism Management at Clemson University. A Fellow in the Strom Thurmond Institute and of the Academy of Leisure Sciences, he was the Clemson University Centennial Professor, 1994-1996. He is also the recipient of the Clemson University Class of '39 Award for Faculty Excellence. He has published in *The Gerontologist, International Journal of Aging and Human Development, Journal of Leisure Research,* and *Leisure Sciences* and has presented papers and workshops at over 50 national, regional, state, and local conferences on topics ranging from intergenerational programs, patterns of outdoor recreation participation by older individuals, the role of humor in long-term care facilities, and constraints to leisure involvement in retirement. In partnership with representatives from the Strom Thurmond Institute, the South Carolina Division on Aging, the

South Carolina Department of Education, and the South Carolina United Way, he recently received a grant to develop a program matching older individuals and at-risk youth in a community service program.

Kenneth F. Backman, PhD, is Research Associate in the Regional Development Group at the Strom Thurmond Institute of Government and Public Policy at Clemson University, where he is also Assistant Professor in the Department of Parks, Recreation, and Tourism Management. He is Associate Editor of *Tourism Analysis, Leisure Sciences,* and *International Journal of Festival Management and Event Tourism.* His current research projects include "The New South Carolinian Study" of in-migrant retirees; "The Travel and Nature Study" of nature-based travelers' perceptions, interests, and motivations; and "The Study of African American Travelers" and their perceptions, interests, attitudes, and motivations. He has published several book chapters as well as more than 25 articles in journals such as *Leisure Sciences, Journal of Applied Recreation Research, Sociological Inquiry,* and *Annals of Tourism Research.* The author of many other publications, including book reviews and technical reports, he is a frequent speaker, who has recently presented on naturebased travel behavior, tourism and community development, population demographics, and the role of folk arts and crafts in tourism. He is a member of the Ecotourism Society, the National Parks and Recreation Association, the Policy Studies Association, and the American Planning Association.

Foreword

The proliferation of intergenerational programs throughout this country speaks well for the future of relationships betwen young and old Americans. The efforts to bring these diverse age groups together have proven succesful in a variety of programs. Although these successful programs often differ in nature and purpose, most share one common characteristic: effective participant training.

Effective training does not happen by chance. It takes a great deal of preparation, planning, and research. Our experiences with a variety of intergenerational programs indicate there are several distinct areas of training needs. In this book we have provided extensive information on each of these areas. The materials in each chapter have been used in actual training programs and will provide intergenerational trainers with a plethora of useful material.

Preparing Paricipants for Intergenerational Interaction: Training for Success includes twelve chapters. Chapter 1 is designed to furnish an overview of intergenerational programs. Chapter 2 provides an extensive description of the program that resulted in most of the materials detailed in the training manual. Howe-To Industries is an intergenerational program based in McCormick, South Carolina. It is designed to teach youth entrepreneurial skills through a mentoring program. Chapter 2 also includes a brief description of other exemplary intergenerational programs. These are identified to provide information on the state of the art of this rapidly growing area. The second chapter concludes with an overview of funding of intergenerational programs. It describes procedures to be followed in seeking support to initiate and sustain intergenerational eforts. Chapter 3 focuses on the evaluation of programs. The role of evaluation, as well as techniques and procedures appropriate to intergenerational programs, will be detailed.

Chapters 4 and 5 focus on Community Awareness and Oral History. These training units were included in this issue to provide both an historical perspective on the community and a contemporary one. These chapters

[Haworth indexing entry note]: "Foreword." Hawkins, Melissa O., and Francis A. McGuire. Published in *Preparing Participants for Intergenerational Interaction: Training for Success* (ed: Melissa O. Hawkins, Francis A. McGuire, and Kenneth F. Backman) The Haworth Press, Inc., 1999, pp. xv-xvi. Single or multiple copies of this article are available for a fee from The Haworth Document Delivery Service [1-800-342-9678, 9:00 a.m. - 5:00 p.m. (EST). E-mail address: getinfo@haworthpressinc.com].

are designed respectively, to familiarize volunteers with the various aspects of their communities and to interview one another about places or potential roles within the community structure. Conclusions drawn from these units will give young and old new perspectives on their community's history, potential for enhancement, and future prospects.

Chapters 6 through 9 focus on increasing participant sensitivity towards others they will encounter as a part of their intergenerational experience. Chapter 6 introduces issues associated with understanding, appreciating, and accommodating differences between people. Chapters 7, 8, and 9 focus on at-risk youth, older adults, and racial and ethnic groups, respectively.

Since intergenerational programs are inherently group focused, there is a need to understand the dynamics required to create effectiveness teams. The focus of Chapters 10 and 11 are devoted to this crucial area. Finally, promotion of intergenerational programs is key to program success and perpetuation. Therefore, Chapter 12 focuses on Marketing techiques and concepts.

Chapter 4 (Community Awareness), Chapter 5 (Oral History), Chapter 7 (Understanding and Mentoring At-Risk Youth), Chapter 8 (Aging Sensitivity), Chapter 9 (Racial and Ethnic Understanding), Chapter 11 (Group Dynamics), and Chapter 12 (Marketing), present specific training modules and follow a similar format. They all include learning objectives, identification of key concepts and terms, and specific exercises, as well as handouts and transparencies to accompany those exercises.

The book concludes with a list of pertinent references and resources. They are designed to provide the trainer with a starting point for further information related to intergenerational programming.

Melissa O. Hawkins
Francis A. McGuire

Acknowledgments

The editors are indebted to the AARP-Andrus Foundation for funding Howe-To Industries and for their support of intergenerational efforts. The editors thank the authors who contributed their work to this publication. They would also like to thank Paul Wright, Katie Johnson, Jennifer Schneider, and Elizabeth Dargle for their careful editing of the training materials. Much thanks also goes to Jean Martin for her clerical assistance. They gratefully acknowledge the efforts of Linda Kidd, the staff at the John de la Howe School, and all the Howe-To Industry participants. In addition, Rich Weston and Jeff Allen, part of the original Howe-To Industries team, have their deepest gratitude. Appreciation is also extended to the folks at the Temple University Center for Intergenerational Learning for their guidance.

Chapter 1

Introduction to Intergenerational Programs

Francis A. McGuire
Melissa O. Hawkins

For centuries the way society conveyed culture, values and the means of survival has been through the enculturation of the young by the elderly. In today's society this process is of enduring importance. However, factors such as increased mobility often limit the interaction of older adults with youths. The networks of economic, educational and cultural interdependence supported by households and neighborhoods composed of grandparents, parents and children have largely disappeared. Job mobility and the breakup of many extended families have changed our society from a "front porch" social system to one defined by generational isolation (Creating Intergenerational Coalitions, 1995). Grandparents often live far away, parents work outside the home, and single parent households are common. Tasks and opportunities that previously drew families together are now handed over to paid professionals, institutions and the government. According to Kaplan (1994) "today's living, learning, and recreation activities separate people according to age. As a result, youth and senior adults share neighborhoods but live in different worlds" (p. 3). An alternate method of fostering interaction between the generations is rapidly becoming part of the American landscape, planned intergenerational programs.

The resources provided by young and old Americans are crucial to the future of the country. There is a need to identify techniques for effectively combining the energy of youth with the experience of the elderly for the

[Haworth co-indexing entry note]: "Introduction to Intergenerational Programs." McGuire, Francis A., and Melissa O. Hawkins. Co-published simultaneously in *Activities, Adaptation & Aging* (The Haworth Press, Inc.) Vol. 23, No. 1, 1998, pp. 1-9; and: *Preparing Participants for Intergenerational Interaction: Training for Success* (ed: Melissa O. Hawkins, Francis A. McGuire, and Kenneth F. Backman) The Haworth Press, Inc., 1999, pp. 1-9. Single or multiple copies of this article are available for a fee from The Haworth Document Delivery Service [1-800-342-9678, 9:00 a.m. - 5:00 p.m. (EST). E-mail address: getinfo@haworthpressinc.com].

1

betterment of the communities in which they reside. As Leiloglolu (1996) wrote: "the historical perspective and experience of old people and the energy and idealism of young people must be linked to deal with the monumental societal problems that endanger our world." Intergeneration- al initiatives provide one such link. These activities create opportunities for interaction between generations and may result in the exchange of values, beliefs, and attitudes between older Americans and their younger counterparts.

In his landmark study entitled *Partners in Growth: Elder Mentors and At-Risk Youth* (1988), Freedman identified the basic principle of intergen- erational programming: older adults provide a largely untapped resource with great amounts of unobligated time that can be used to help youth. The premise is deceptively simple. It implies that bringing young and old together will result in a mutually beneficial arrangement. Older adults will find fulfillment in the role of mentor to needy young people and the young will have access to positive role models sharing knowledge and experi- ence because of their contact with mature adults. The promise and poten- tial for such interactions seem boundless. However, as Freedman's work documents, the premise and the promise are often lost in the operational- ization of intergenerational programs. The reality is that successful inter- generational programs require careful planning and preparation of all in- volved parties if they are to succeed. The purpose of this monograph is to provide information needed to develop successful programs.

A BRIEF HISTORY OF INTERGENERATIONAL PROGRAMS

The idea of bringing together young people and older adults in inter- generational programs is not new. Lutz and Haller (1996) indicated that intergenerational programming has evolved into a distinct field, with a wide range of projects, over the past twenty years.

The roots of the current trend toward intergenerational programs can be traced to the 1960s when the federal government established the Foster Grandparent program. The Adopt a Grandparent Program was developed in 1963 at the University of Florida, and Serve and Enrich Retirement by Volunteer Experience (SERVE) was established in New York. These programs provided the impetus for the develop- ment of the Retired Senior Volunteer Program (RSVP) in 1969. The 1970s and 1980s marked the development of several new intergenera- tional programs and initiatives (see Newman, 1989, for a review). The University of Pittsburgh established Generations Together in 1979 and Temple University established The Center for Intergenerational

Learning one year later. These two university-based centers continue to serve as clearinghouses for intergenerational resources. In the 1980s the emphasis of the National Council on Aging was on the "creation of strategies for linking individuals over the age of 60 with youths under 25." Generations United was founded in 1986, by more than 100 national organizations, to increase public awareness about issues faced by Americans of all ages. Generations United promotes programs which increase intergenerational cooperation and exchange. Generations United also participates in attempts to bring generations together in service to one another and to the community (Scannell & Roberts, 1994). In the 1990s the National Recreation and Parks Association initiated a major effort to increase the use of intergenerational programs in recreation agencies.

Since their genesis in the 1960s intergenerational programs have become accepted, and in fact expected, components in the comprehensive mix of programs for older individuals. A variety of groups, including school-age children, latch key children, children with disabilities and at-risk youths have been included in the variety of intergenerational programs.

DESCRIPTION OF INTERGENERATIONAL PROGRAMS

The landscape of intergenerational programs is marked by diversity. There are programs of every sort, sharing only one commonality, the mix of young and old. According to Friedman (1996) there are several intergenerational program models. These include:

1. Youths serving older adults–These are programs that bring younger individuals into contact with older adults through the provision of a service. For example, youths may install smoke detectors in the homes of older individuals, visit long term care facilities or visit older people who are confined to their homes.
2. Older adults serving youths–This model involves older individuals providing a service to their younger counterparts. One of the most common programs of this type is homework assistance with elderly helping children complete assignments and providing tutoring. Other programs include working with pregnant teens, assisting in child care centers and developing job skills in adolescents.
3. Young and old serving the community–Programs of service such as building playgrounds, intergenerational crime watch programs, and community beautification efforts fall into this category.

Intergenerational programs are not defined by their content. In fact, the foci of the programs are as diverse as the communities where they occur, since community needs should determine program direction. The essential ingredient shared by all intergenerational programs is the beneficial merging of the young and the old in a planned program of service.

BENEFITS OF INTERGENERATIONAL PROGRAMS TO ADULTS

The advantages of participation in intergenerational programs have been well documented (Freedman, 1988). Scannell and Roberts (1994) list several benefits older adults may receive from involvement in intergenerational programs. These include opportunities to:

- remain productive members of society;
- use skills accrued over a lifetime in new ways;
- interact successfully with young people;
- develop new friendships;
- have new experiences;
- decrease loneliness and isolation.

DeBoard and Flanagan (1994) suggest intergenerational programs also offer older volunteers the opportunity to achieve a sense of fulfillment by passing on life experiences and skills to others. In addition, there is an opportunity to earn extra income or make a valuable volunteer contribution.

Leiloglolu (1996) identified several benefits from involvement in intergenerational programs. These include increased personal and social adjustment, enhanced life satisfaction and increased feelings of well-being. In addition, older participants in intergenerational programs experience increased levels of activity and industry and an opportunity to give and receive love.

The opportunity to serve as a mentor and role model to a young person can be the catalyst for experiencing the multitude of benefits identified above. However, the value of intergenerational programs is in the exchange relationship between young and old. As a result, young participants also benefit from their involvement with older adults.

BENEFITS OF INTERGENERATIONAL PROGRAMS TO YOUTH

A variety of justifications have been provided for intergenerational programs with adolescents. Cherry, Benest, Gates, and White (1985) claimed adolescents and elderly share a variety of needs and characteristics. Therefore, many benefits experienced by the older participants in intergenerational programs are also identified as positive outcomes for the young participants.

Youths' access to adults, particularly older adults, is frequently limited. This is unfortunate since older adults, including grandparents, can play a unique and valuable role in the development of youth.

Intergenerational programs provide youth with adult role models willing to share their experience and maturity. Older adults can serve as effective mentors to youths helping them deal with the problems and crises experienced during an often difficult time of life. The mentor may be the only older individual to whom a young person can turn for encouragement and advice.

Programs bringing young and old together can also assist in the development of social, academic and work skills in youths. The contact with individuals who are willing to share a lifetime of skills may be crucial to the later life success of the youths involved in intergenerational programs. Scannell and Roberts (1994) view intergenerational programs as giving youths an opportunity to gain awareness and appreciation of the aging process while dispelling stereotypes about older adults. As Freedman (1988) concluded, ". . . all these relationships appear to help change a life trajectory from one headed for failure to a more adaptive path of survival."

CHARACTERISTICS OF SUCCESSFUL INTERGENERATIONAL PROGRAMS

The components of successful intergenerational programs are no different from the factors that are necessary for success in any program. A clear mission is a necessity. The purpose should be clear to all individuals involved in the project. There is a need for careful recruitment, selection and placement of the participants.

Since the older participants are typically volunteers, the same procedures used in any volunteer program should be in place. There should be job descriptions, clearly explaining roles, duties and limits. Volunteers should know what is expected of them and how they will be used in the program.

An effective recruitment program must be instituted. Fischer and Schaffer (1993) examined the research related to recruiting older volunteers to determine what techniques are most effective. They concluded that a systematic method of recruiting new volunteers through personal solicitation is crucial for all volunteer programs. Personal solicitation includes using current volunteers to identify potential volunteers as well as recruiting through existing organizations. However, they also concluded that recruiting solely through personal contacts is not sufficient if the program is to continue to grow. Building volunteer recruitment entirely on personal contacts may result in volunteers coming only from a narrowly defined population. Fisher and Schaffer (1993) found that media-based recruitment can be effective if the messages fit the interests and motivations of the targeted audience. Programs seeking to expand their population of potential volunteers tend to use media-based recruitment techniques. A multiphase volunteer recruitment effort relying on several approaches will be the most effective campaign. In addition, it is easier to recruit volunteers who already have community ties, such as prior volunteer experience, attachment to community organizations such as churches or social organizations, or have been long time residents of a community. Therefore, initial volunteer efforts may be focused on individuals with attachment to their community.

Recruiting volunteers is crucial to the success of most intergenerational programs. However, recruitment is only effective if it is married to retention. Turnover in volunteers is to be expected and is part of a cycle. Most volunteers will leave the program at some point. Nevertheless, older volunteers are a highly committed group and continue to volunteer for a long period (Fischer & Schaffer, 1993). Retention strategies can be effective in retaining volunteers for as long as feasible.

The research on retention points toward several approaches that will maximize the likelihood volunteers will continue in a program (Fischer & Schaffer, 1993). The initial step in ensuring retention is selectivity in volunteer recruitment. Targeting individuals who have prior volunteer experience, who are motivated by a desire to help others and are well matched with their assigned duties will assist in retention. Once volunteers are recruited and placed, successful experiences further enhance commitment. Training and preparation of volunteers will increase the likelihood of success.

There are some unique aspects of intergenerational programs that require attention if they are to succeed. There must be a balance between the costs and benefits older adults accrue because of their involvement. According to Antonucci (1990), reciprocity is a "basic aspect of normal well-functioning support networks" (p. 211). Reciprocity requires that a balance between rewards and costs be experienced by all parties in an interaction. If one party receives more rewards than he or she provides then the relationship is not reciprocal. Therefore, if intergenerational programs are to succeed, there must be reciprocity between older adults and younger partners in the relationship. Such a balanced relationship requires all participants receive benefits as well as incurring costs from their involvement. There must be real, as opposed to contrived, opportunities to contribute to the well-being of others while at the same time there must be opportunities to reap the benefits of involvement. Mentoring and partnering are ways to build reciprocity into intergenerational programs.

Older adults may have limitations that must be taken into account in intergenerational programs. For example, individuals living on a fixed income may need to be reimbursed for expenses resulting from their involvement. Transportation or health related problems may also be present and require accommodations. Potential volunteers may be concerned that too many demands will be placed on their time and impinge on their freedom. Other volunteers may be available at only certain times of the year since they may travel in the winter or take extended trips to visit friends or family. Scheduling should allow for these absences.

Lutz and Haller (1996) analyzed data from a 1994-1995 survey conducted by the National Council on Aging Family Friends Resource Center which included information from 150 intergenerational projects. They were able to identify nine elements considered critical to the success of intergenerational projects. These "best practice" elements included:

1. Community need–The assessment of community need forms the basis for the planning and implementation of projects. Documenting and specifying areas of community need is crucial to success.
2. Community involvement–Community involvement is necessary to facilitate volunteer recruitment, secure financial support, and locate technical expertise. Involvement as early in the project as feasible, through, for example, the establishment of an advisory board, pays dividends later in the program.
3. Project planning and development–Developing a plan with goals, specific objectives, tasks and needed resources helps focus the program and keep it on track.
4. Motivated volunteers–Volunteers are the backbone of any intergenerational program. They are the single most important resource. Finding ways to motivate them is crucial to success. The motivation of volunteers begins in the recruitment stage when enthusiasm and commitment can be fostered. Training, monitoring,

supporting, and recognizing volunteers are also necessary to keep them motivated. There are many excellent publications detailing methods for recruiting and retaining volunteers (Ellis, 1994; Fisher & Cole, 1993; McCurley & Vineyard, 1988; Schiman & Lordeman, 1989; Vineyard, 1984). The information from these is too extensive to include in this publication. However, it is strongly recommended they be consulted before initiating an intergenerational program.

5. Cooperating organizations–Most intergenerational projects involve many agencies in local communities. Programs will require cooperation between entities serving the elderly, such as offices on aging and retiree groups, and youth, such as schools and recreation agencies. The resources provided by these organizations are most useful if a cooperative model is developed.

6. Gifted staff–Most intergenerational programs have few paid staff. A typical model includes one paid staff in a coordinating role. The skills of this individual will determine the success of the program. Organization, communication and administrative abilities are essential. Successful staff will be effective in motivating volunteers and galvanizing the local community to action.

7. Accountability–Participants, funders, and the community require information about the progress a project is making. Records related to volunteer hours, activity performance and administrative procedures assist in establishing accountability.

8. Public relations–Information about successful programs should be shared with the public. Dissemination allows replication and therefore spreads the impact of good programs beyond the confines of the communities where they are conducted. Public relations also help recruit new volunteers and build community support.

9. Evaluation–Programs are improved through an ongoing assessment process. Identifying the effective and ineffective component of a program allows increased efficacy and efficiency. In addition, evaluation helps develop successful approaches that can be shared with other communities.

We suggest adding a tenth ingredient for success to the above list. Successful programs require training of participants. This may be particularly the case in intergenerational programs. Integrating young and old into a program is not a simple process. Proximity with individuals from a different age group is not sufficient to bring about bonding and effective interaction. Efforts specifically designed to facilitate integration are needed. There is a need for training programs designed to inform the young about the old and the elderly about the young. The stereotypes held by each group must be explored and addressed. This is crucial to the success of intergenerational programs.

Chapter 2

Exemplary Intergenerational Programs

Melissa O. Hawkins
Francis A. McGuire

The proliferation of intergenerational efforts has yielded a variety of models useful in determining program direction. There are hundreds of programs that can provide a starting point for agencies and communities seeking to find ways of bringing the young and old together. As shown in Chapter 1, one way to categorize programs is based on the focus of service: young and old in service to their community; elderly serving the young; or, young providing service to older individuals. The purpose of this chapter is to describe illustrative intergenerational programs in each of these areas. This brief overview provides a starting point for individuals desirous of initiating programs such as those described.

Initiating an intergenerational program requires more than a good idea. Most intergenerational programs rely on public as well as private funding as they develop. Locating and securing necessary financial resources is crucial to the survival of intergenerational programs. Therefore, an overview of potential funding sources is provided at the end of this chapter.

YOUNG AND OLD IN SERVICE TO THE COMMUNITY

This approach to intergenerational activity is probably the fastest growing model. There are a variety of programs in which young and old

[Haworth co-indexing entry note]: "Exemplary Intergenerational Programs." Hawkins, Melissa O., and Francis A. McGuire. Co-published simultaneously in *Activities, Adaptation & Aging* (The Haworth Press, Inc.) Vol. 23, No. 1, 1998, pp. 11-25; and: *Preparing Participants for Intergenerational Interaction: Training for Success* (ed: Melissa O. Hawkins, Francis A. McGuire, and Kenneth F. Backman) The Haworth Press, Inc., 1999, pp. 11-25. Single or multiple copies of this article are available for a fee from The Haworth Document Delivery Service [1-800-342-9678, 9:00 a.m. - 5:00 p.m. (EST). E-mail address: getinfo@haworthpressinc.com].

11

coalesce around services provided to their community. Initiatives include projects designed to join young and old in building community recreation facilities such as swimming pools, beautifying parks, creating community oral histories, and establishing community gardens.

One such project, Howe-To Industries, brings young and old together in an entrepreneurship model. The authors of this monograph established Howe-To Industries with support from the AARP-Andrus Foundation. Howe-To Industries incorporate many principles outlined in Chapter 1 and provides a strong model for the development of intergenerational programs. Therefore, an extensive description of this program is given below. It is followed by briefer descriptions of several other projects. They document the rich diversity in intergenerational programming. The reader will discover a wealth of approaches useful for determining the focus of an intergenerational effort.

Howe-To Industries

In 1987 a Memorandum of Agreement was signed between Clemson University and the John de la Howe School, a state supported residential school for at-risk adolescents. This agreement established a number of cooperative activities including educational, research, and operational programs. The Enterprise Market Program (EMP) was one important result of the memorandum. Within the structure of the EMP, the youth at de la Howe established a student-run public market in the school's renovated dairy barn, selecting and marketing their own products, handling bookkeeping and expenses, and distributing profits among student workers. The Strom Thurmond Institute and departments at Clemson University including the Architecture, Management, and Parks, Recreation and Tourism Management, were integral to the success of the EMP. Faculty and students were involved in barn, grounds, and outbuilding renovation, business development, and therapeutic recreation benefit planning.

In January 1993, efforts by staff at the Strom Thurmond Institute and the Department of Parks, Recreation and Tourism Management at Clemson University allowed an expansion of the Enterprise Market Program at John de la Howe. By obtaining a three-year grant from the AARP Andrus Foundation, the "Intergenerational Entrepreneurship Demonstration Project" (IEDP) was established. Older adults of McCormick County were added into the structure of the EMP through the IEDP. McCormick County's long time residents and new retirees to the area serve side by side as volunteer mentors to the at-risk youth at John de la Howe. Though outside funding has ended, the market continues to operate out of the renovated dairy barn at the school and is now known as "Howe-To Industries."

Older mentors in Howe-To Industries offer diversity in skills, experiences, and backgrounds. Most of the "newcomers" to McCormick are in-migrant retirees to the county's recently established retirement community, Savannah Lakes Village. They are generally well educated and from affluent backgrounds. The other mentors are long time residents of McCormick County. Many of these older adults are minorities and from a different economic stratum than Savannah Lakes Village residents. Together the two groups give the students at John de la Howe a broad base from which to learn and receive guidance.

With assistance from their mentors, disadvantaged youths produce goods to sell in their own country market. By sharing their accumulated life experiences, the older mentors serve as support figures while introducing the ideas of small business development to the underprivileged "potential achievers" at the John de la Howe School. An additional benefit is that the older adults, who are from diverse backgrounds, are establishing meaningful relationships with one another, thus enhancing the sense of community in McCormick.

Project Objectives

In establishing the objectives for Howe-To Industries, great emphasis was placed on melding the two diverse groups of older adult volunteers in McCormick. Therefore, community building was the first objective. This objective and the objectives of encouraging interaction and integration, and building social networks, were approached through similar methods. Methods included ongoing training, offering opportunities to take on various roles in the project, and holding events such as an annual "Barn Yard Bash" volunteer recruitment party and bimonthly appreciation luncheons.

Other objectives included increasing community awareness; properly and successfully training, recruiting, and monitoring participants; encouraging personal development; conveying business skills; mutual sharing and learning among participants; and offering role models to the youth in the project. These objectives were and continue to be accomplished through many measures including eight, ongoing training modules and one to one mentoring. The unique organizational structure of Howe-To Industries also facilitates meeting objectives by offering opportunities for participants to be together in the project during committee and company meetings, and during work in the barn market.

Benefits

The benefits of Howe-To Industries are experienced at each level of participation in the project. For example, the youths and older adults have experienced improved attitudes toward each other, increased community involvement and appreciation, and received a great deal of recognition for their efforts. Besides its social benefits and emotional appeal, Howe-To Industries has a practical, educational emphasis. The older adult mentors, youth, and school staff work in Howe-To Industries to develop, produce and sell many different products in their own country market. The school's renovated dairy barn houses the market.

Organizational Structure

The Howe-To Industries organizational structure is functional, yet simplistic. Therefore, it can be easily replicated in other settings. A policy board includes representatives from agencies at the county and state level. There are also an executive committee and a board of directors made up of staff, volunteers and youth. In addition, each participant in Howe-To Industries has the opportunity to join one of the businesses' six working committees: accounting; staffing and transportation; product involvement; activities and events; training and evaluation; and quality control.

Participants have divided themselves into six different companies within Howe-To Industries based on the twelve housing units at John de la Howe. Each of the six companies has its own unique product focus. For example, the Exchange Company focuses on Greenhouse Operation, Quilting, and Seasonal Candy Pots. Other companies are the C and C Company which is in charge of Barn Grounds Beautification and the Barn seasonal bulletin board display; the HAS Company which participates in the "Adopt-A-Highway" Clean-Up, and making Wood Products; the P & N Limited which gathers and sells pine straw, makes pottery and maintains the school's orchard; the Caroville Company which has a vegetable garden, and harvests hay and peanuts; and the Classic Touch Company which is in charge of catfish production, needlework projects, and making birdhouses. The older adult volunteers are evenly assigned among the six companies and work directly with the youths an average of three to five hours per week. School staff participate as well using their expertise in teaching, counseling, and project management.

Company Operations

Company operations began once the organizational structure was established and several planning meetings had taken place involving all of the participants. Initially a start up fund was provided for each company. This was given in a line of credit to allow the companies to purchase supplies. The debt was paid once the companies earned enough profit.

Companies generate ideas for their products or services, and choose the prices they wish to charge. They were taught to consider the potential profits and also the loss risks involved in operating a business. They then create a prototype if feasible and propose their idea to the product involvement committee of Howe-To Industries. If accepted, companies contract with Howe-To Industries to produce and deliver a designated quantity of their product to the market. Similar contracts are made for services. Companies then do the required work and sell the product to Howe-To Industries. Howe-To Industries increases the price of the product by ten to twenty per cent and sells it to the public through the barn market. Profits of Howe-To Industries go back to companies and are used for outings, pizza parties, and other special activities.

Volunteer Roles

The older volunteers fill a variety of roles within the Howe-To Industries Project. Not only do they provide invaluable mentoring contributions but they also assist in generating policies and ideas through work on one of the six operational committees. In addition to these roles, volunteers have become "Company Advisors" involved with the youth in the production of goods or services for the market; "Market Sales Associates" operating the market with the youth during its working hours; or "Lifeshare Instructors," sharing creative and performing arts talents to give community performances. The older mentors have diverse occupational backgrounds providing the youths exposure to a vast array of marketable skills. For instance, a retired banker is teaching the youths basic accounting and bookkeeping skills; a retired carpenter is instructing interested students in the fine art of wood-working; a retired actor is passing on his theatrical expertise; and other talented volunteers are teaching creative pursuits such as needlework, basket-weaving, knitting, and quilt making.

Flexibility, choice, and the variety of roles in the project offer much freedom to the volunteer adults and the youths. In addition, and perhaps most important, the at-risk students are given opportunities to learn responsibility and business and life skills from committed adults who care for them. Benefits of this attention and responsibility are increased self-esteem, and an appreciation of honest, hard work. Additionally, the presence of energetic youth and committed adults contribute to a revitalization of McCormick and an increased sense of community between program participants and Howe-To Industries customers.

Training Component

One unique characteristic of this intergenerational project is its comprehensive training component. (The Training Manual that comprises a major portion of this monograph was developed for training participants in Howe-To Industries.) Before the inception of the program, older mentors, staff and students were provided the opportunity to meet with professional trainers to help prepare them for their duties in Howe-To Industries. The proper training of volunteers is a key component of the process involved in most beneficially managing people who will be helping advance or enhance a cause. Training is especially necessary when volunteers will be working in a preestablished structure such as a school. Training helped to ease the transition for the older adults entering the Howe-To Industries program. It helped the school staff learn what to expect from and how to work with their new assistants. Additionally, the youths, most of whom had experienced few positive interactions with older adults were enlightened about what older people have to offer.

Simply placing people in proximity to one another is not enough. In Howe-To Industries, the most beneficial and productive use of volunteers has come because of training. Training is one way that volunteers receive the message that their work is valued and that they are important. Additional ways this message is conveyed include the bimonthly volunteer appreciation and networking luncheons, and a Howe-To Industries newsletter dedicated totally to volunteer efforts and accomplishments.

Howe-To Industries participants were trained in group dynamics, marketing, working with at-risk youths, community awareness, first aid, oral history, ethnic sensitivity and aging sensitivity. The purpose of the training sessions was to offer an overview and a basic orientation to the project, while teaching both students and volunteers skills that would better equip them to function as interacting teams and business entrepreneurs within Howe-To Industries.

Lessons from Howe-To Industries

Howe-To Industries is a comprehensive, school-based, intergenerational volunteer program. This section is devoted to the key issues that are essential for successful model replication. Many of these issues were also discussed in Chapter 1. The Howe-To Industries experience supports their role in contributing to program success.

Volunteer Recruitment

The best and most qualified person to recruit volunteers is a volunteer. This can be said for recruiting volunteers of all ages. A volunteer can tell potential volunteers about the program in which they will possibly be helping. Other good recruiters of older adult volunteers are other older adults. In fact volunteers of all ages are more easily recruited by peers. Volunteering may become more attractive to an older adult who sees someone who is similar in age, life experiences, and potentially other ways, enjoying the volunteer experience.

Another suggestion for recruiting older adult volunteers is having youths invite them to participate. Older adults may be attracted to a volunteer program if they meet a young person who is involved. Meeting a youth may awaken older adults' desire to be with young people again, or they may realize that they have experiences and skills that they would like to share with the younger generation.

In Howe-To Industries, the project director made the first volunteer recruitment efforts. A dynamic, sincere project director can also persuade older adults to volunteer. Often the enthusiasm of the Director can be contagious, and a wonderful motivator for seniors to use their energy to work with youth.

When deciding where to recruit, the people recruiting must ask themselves what kind of people they are looking for and where those people can be found. For example, if one wants to recruit business leaders, he or she should look at community business clubs, service organizations, and businesses themselves. In Howe-To Industries, recruiting older adults was the goal. Common places to find older adults include senior centers, health fairs, retirement housing, meetings of retired professionals, AARP meetings, and church events. Some older adults pick up their grandchildren at school or day care. They can be approached for recruitment at those places, too.

In Howe-To Industries, school staff at John de la Howe was already in place since the volunteer program was integrated into the school curriculum through the Enterprise Market Program. Suggestions for staff in intergenerational programs include teachers, recreation therapists, counselors, support staff, and recreation professionals. The school staff at John de la Howe provided a bridge between the old and the young involved in Howe-To Industries, due to their unique relationships with the students and desire to make the volunteers feel appreciated.

Suggestions of where to find youths for intergenerational programs include the public school system, church youth groups, community centers, recreation programs, and service learning classes. In addition, some youths may be identified through the judicial or social service systems.

The methods used to recruit volunteers vary, and many of them should be employed to reach a broad audience. Word of mouth is usually a method that insures that people will hear about a volunteer program. Notification should be given to community leaders of all ages, active seniors, and ministers. Anyone who will listen should be informed and asked if they will help spread the word, too. Promotional flyers are also very helpful and should be placed everywhere possible. They should be bright but tasteful and give brief information about the volunteer program, as well as whom to contact about finding out more. Newspaper advertisements may also be effective in recruiting participants. Finally, publicity can also be obtained through church and community newsletters.

There are two approaches to volunteer recruitment–recruitment by groups and one-to-one recruitment. One-to-one recruitment promotes greater understanding and potential volunteers are more likely to ask questions when they have a recruiter's full attention. A community get together is suggested to introduce the volunteer program to older adults. At this get together, testimonials by current volunteers or youth can impact the potential volunteers. Later, the Project Director can follow-up with people who attended the function and try to recruit on a one-to-one personal level. Some people may sign up to volunteer at the group event. In Howe-To Industries, the annual "Barn Yard Bash" volunteer recruitment party was successful in obtaining on the spot volunteers as well as those who needed some nurturing.

It is important that anyone who wants to volunteer be interviewed and "screened." This process reveals people's talents and professional backgrounds. All volunteers are not necessarily beneficial to intergenerational programs. If a volunteer does not add to the program, and help advance it to reach the program's goal, then she or he has no place in it and should be reassigned or dismissed.

Volunteer Retention

To insure a successful volunteer program, a significant number of volunteers have to stay involved in the program. The retention of volunteers in an intergenerational program revolves around the consideration of the needs of older people. Some of these needs may be unique to the older adult age group.

Older people need respect and feelings of usefulness. They are experiencing a time in their lives when many roles are lost or are changing. These roles include employee, friend, and spouse. For the first time in their lives, they may be unsure of what they plan to do in the future. In America's youth-oriented culture, the self-esteem of older adults may suffer. It is important to empower volunteers, listen to their suggestions and act on them.

Training is essential for volunteer retention. It must be fun, and it must be tailored to meet the needs of the program. Training in areas such as group dynamics, first-aid, and aging sensitivity should take place. Youths, older adults, and staff should be trained in separate groups at first. They should first get to know each other within their homogeneous groups. Next they should be trained together. This will help them ease into their new relationships. Then when asked to actually work together in the volunteer program they will have already had the opportunity to interact in the training sessions.

Also necessary for volunteer retention are clearly written job descriptions for volunteers. The job for the volunteer must be well defined, including the title of the position, expectations for the volunteer, and scheduling. Job descriptions are also especially helpful when paid staff is involved in the volunteer program. Job descriptions will aid both the volunteers and the staff in understanding their roles in the program, thus reducing chances for potential conflict.

Volunteer Recognition

A final key to retaining volunteers is planning thoughtful volunteer recognition efforts. Recognition is another human need that is a vital component to working with older adult volunteers. Volunteers can be recognized according to the number of hours served, an outstanding job on something, or as reported by others. Methods to recognize volunteers include newspaper publicity, project newsletters, personal notes, a plaque in the facility where the program operates, and personal gift plaques. Appreciation luncheons or drop-ins are also suggested. These can serve to recognize volunteers and in monitoring or evaluating the volunteer program.

Issues Involving Paid Staff

The work of the volunteers must contribute to the achievement of organizational goals. For the volunteer program to make a difference, the right volunteers must be matched with appropriate responsibilities. The volunteers and paid staff must work together in the pursuit of common goals. This joint pursuit is fundamental to the success of any volunteer program. Also integral to program success is the development of volunteer positions that relate directly to the organization's mission and that build positive staff/volunteer relations. Friction between these two groups diverts valuable time and energy from organization goals. Volunteer job descriptions should be developed in two phases. In Phase I, an organization must examine the tasks that could best be done by volunteer staff in light of its mission, organizational structure, and personnel policies. In Phase II, specific volunteer positions and position guidelines should be developed with clear job descriptions. Specific job descriptions are important because they delineate a distinction between volunteer role and staff role. It is important that staff are recognized, appreciated, fully informed, and included in everything that the volunteers are. Treating paid staff with the same appreciation as volunteers will aid in avoiding hurt feelings, misunderstandings, and miscommunications.

Youth and Elderly Against Crime

An additional program that demonstrates young and old in service to the community is the Youth and Elderly Against Crime program in Miami, Florida. Cited as a Point of Light by President George Bush, the program was created in 1990 as part of Dade County's Intergenerational Law Advocacy Program. Youth and Elderly Against Crime was designed to promote cooperation between young and old as they strive to improve the quality of life in the Miami area (*Intergenerational Projects Idea Book,* 1993).

Participants go through extensive training and preparation before they serve the community by drafting resolutions and policy statements to improve public policy, lobby legislators, and perform educational skits about crime prevention in the Miami area. Students from nine area schools are enrolled in social studies, civics, criminal justice, or government classes that participate in the program. These schools have "adopted" senior citizen groups or public housing residents in their neighborhoods to identify and solve community problems ("Teenagers + Senior Citizens = Crime-busting Combination," 1992; "Youth and Elderly Team Up," 1990).

Students begin the program by listening to speakers from local advocacy groups who are knowledgeable about crime as it affects both the young and the old. Students also attend public forums and legislature meetings which deal with crime-related issues. Strategy seminars at which students, seniors, and teachers discuss problems and develop communication skills are held at the school several times a year. Each summer, old and young project participants also attend a four-day institute at Florida International University to discuss crime issues with law enforcement officers, and various community leaders and advocacy groups. Here they draft legislative proposals and lobby legislators who attend the institute.

Students and senior citizen groups are matched and develop task forces in their communities. Police officers, community leaders, and educators participate in the task forces as they develop plans for improving their neighborhoods. Several times a year, task forces meet with city officials, legislators, and the community at large to introduce their proposals. Intergenerational teams are also given the opportunity to present their proposals to committees during the legislative session in the state capital.

Activities of the intergenerational teams have included writing legislation for stiffer penalties for crimes committed near elderly residences and the creation of a "safe zone" for the elderly. As a result of community surveys by the teams, additional lights have been installed in numerous locations around elderly housing. Safety workshops which include crime prevention techniques and skits depicting crime scenes have been conducted in Miami neighborhoods, educating both young and old in the Miami area.

Both Howe-To Industries and Youth and Elderly Against Crime involve active older adults working with young people to serve their communities. Benefits of such programs are witnessed by individuals of all ages in the communities where they operate. Replication of such programs is encouraged in order to bridge gaps between the generations and place the old and young in positions to improve the community for everyone.

OLDER ADULTS SERVING YOUTH

There are many programs designed to provide adult intervention into the lives of youth. Many of these programs involve older adults in a mentoring relationship with needy children. The mentoring often focuses on health or education needs as well as socialization and companionship. The three programs described below typify the "service to youth" model of intergenerational programming.

Apple-A-Day Preschool

Newton, Kansas is home to an intergenerational program based on elderly meeting the needs of the young. Newton Presbyterian Manor, a retirement community, is the site of the Apple-A-Day Preschool, the first preschool in Kansas housed within a retirement community. The preschool "has provided unprecedented intergenerational programming for residents of the retirement community, and is also meeting a real community need. As an added bonus, the preschool's operation has provided Presbyterian Manor with a source of revenue." The idea for the preschool originated when one of two such facilities in Newton closed, leaving the community underserved. The first step in its development was the process of obtaining the necessary clearances from various state agencies. The next step was determining the best location for the facility. It was housed in the Manor's recreation room at first. However, completion of a wellness center at the Manor allowed the preschool to move into a room that had been used for physical therapy. Costs were reduced by purchasing equipment for the preschool for $1,850 from the school that had closed.

There is a great deal of interaction between the children and the older adults of Newton Manor. The health care residents, as well as residents in the special care unit and in assisted living, interact with the children on a daily basis. Six residents serve as foster grandparents. Other residents greet the children in the lobby every morning.

The marriage of Newton Manor and the Apple-A-Day Preschool not only provides a meaningful activity for the residents. It also yields approximately $8,000 in revenue annually. In addition, the entire Newton community benefits from the services provided (Elmore, 1996).

Phone Pal

Phone Pal is an award winning program designed to use older adults to meet the needs of latch key children. The free program started in 1989 in Cowley County, Kansas and was sponsored by the County Council on Aging. Thirty older adults are paired with 64 children who are alone before or after school. Volunteers and children are matched according to interests and personality. Volunteers are carefully screened and trained. A part-time paid coordinator runs the program. This individual is crucial to its success. The adults call their phone pal before or after school, and sometimes both, to provide encouragement and support. All the participants, including children, siblings, parents and Phone Pals, come together at Halloween, Christmas and at a spring party to have fun and become better acquainted (KIN Intergenerational Excellence Awards, 1996).

Seniors for Childhood Immunization

This project, in Denton County and Dallas County, Texas, uses older volunteers to provide families with at-risk children information on preventive health care and immunization. The goal of the project (Lutz & Haller, 1996, p. 14) is to improve immunizations rates by:

- educating new mothers in hospitals about preschool immunization;
- enrolling mothers in immunization reminder programs;
- calling or sending cards to remind mothers of scheduled immunizations;
- scanning immunization records and reminding parents whose children are behind in immunizations.

Two locations house the project, a hospital and a community clinic. The average age of the volunteer staff is 71. In addition to sending postcards and making phone calls, volunteers also greet children when they come in for immunizations, read stories to them, and visit new mothers to describe the importance of immunizations. Volunteers commit an average of eight hours per month to the program and receive 20 hours of training as well as semiannual in-service programs. In addition to the volunteers, an administrator leads each local project (Lutz & Haller, 1996).

YOUTH SERVING OLDER ADULTS

Many intergenerational programs are designed to allow the young participants to serve their older counterparts while also receiving assistance. However, programs focusing exclusively on youth serving the elderly are relatively rare. Those that exist appear to emphasize visitation by the young to long term care facilities and senior centers to interact with older residents and participants. In addition, there are programs in which older youths provide services such as home maintenance to older individuals. Two programs from Temple University's Center for Intergenerational Learning exemplify the role younger people can play in the lives of the elderly. A brief description of these programs will provide insight into the types of services youth can provide.

Telefriends

The Telefriends program in Delaware County, Pennsylvania, brings older individuals and high school volunteers together through the telephone. The project grew out of a need by homebound elderly for companionship and telephone reassurance. The project, supported by the local school district and Temple University's Center for Intergenerational Learning, as well as community service programs for the aging and local churches, matches school students with an older partner. The youths receive academic credit for their participation. They also are trained in communication skills, aging sensitivity and interviewing techniques. Telefriends talk on the telephone twice a week during the school day. Bell Atlantic and two unions, the Communication Workers of America, and the International Brotherhood of Electrical Workers, support the project (Center for Intergenerational Learning, 1996a).

Time Out Respite Care

The Time Out Respite Care Program began in 1988 in Montgomery County, Pennsylvania. The Pew Memorial Trust funds the project that operates in Philadelphia County. Students from local colleges are recruited to provide temporary relief for individuals caring for frail older adults. The respite care allows caregivers temporarily to escape the stress of daily care for a loved one. The student respite workers receive 10 hours of training on topics including caregiving issues, Alzheimer's Disease, normal aging, providing a safe environment, recreational activities, and dealing with loss and grief. The respite workers provide recreational activities during their visit to the individual's home. They also prepare meals and snacks, provide bathroom assistance and support caregivers in any way possible. However, they do not administer medication or provide personal care. The families using the respite workers are charged $6.00 per hour and commit to at least eight hours per month (Center for Intergenerational Learning, 1996b).

Funding for Intergenerational Programs

The programs described are suggestive of the variety of needs that can be met through intergenerational programs. The creation of an intergenerational force combining knowledge and enthusiasm will provide a resource that any community can use. However, the development of an intergenerational program will usually involve costs. The remainder of this chapter will focus on raising funds to support intergenerational efforts.

Finding the funds to operate an intergenerational program may not be as difficult as it seems. It should be noted that resources for project operation do not have to be in the form of cash. Contributions of project materials and supplies, personnel time, activity space, food, publicity, and transportation assistance are excellent sources of support in an intergenerational program. Additionally, relationships with groups who make such "in-kind" donations can be nurtured for future gifts, including gifts of cash.

If immediate funding is needed for the program, however, there are a number of options. Funds can be obtained through grants from private, public, and state entities, as well as the federal government. Many private foundations have serving youths, serving the elderly, or educational initiatives as their funding foci. There are state and national foundations. For a foundation listing, refer to *The Foundation Directory,* in the local library.

Both the federal and the state governments have money designated for specific programs. Like foundations, foci include a variety of subjects including youths and older adults. Others address specific needs of the nation and the state for a given time period. For example, currently the federal and state departments of education have funds for specific types of educational initiatives, such as service learning and preparation for employment. Money is also available through other federal and state departments. *The Federal Register* is the source for obtaining information on federal grant opportunities. State agencies can be contacted directly. Local community administrative departments may also have grant funds for community development or improvements as well.

Funds can also be obtained through donations from individuals and local businesses. Donations in the form of cash or supplies are obviously helpful. Donations can come from churches, hardware stores, craft stores, food establishments, or community members. Intergenerational projects are very attractive and many people and agencies are willing to help in varying degrees. For large corporate donations refer to the *Corporate Giving Directory*.

Soliciting funds involves a balance between being assertive and respectful for the potential donor. Most foundations and corporations publish guidelines that outline how they wish to be approached. Requesting these guidelines requires only a phone call. Additionally, the aforementioned directories contain information on how to approach foundations and corporations. Good judgment is needed when approaching individuals or local businesses. Sincerity and belief in the importance of intergenerational programs will be the convincing factor. Bringing program participants to meet with potential funders so that they may discuss the benefits of the intergenerational program will make the abstract concept of giving money a more realistic, understandable idea, and seeing the program beneficiaries will make helping the program hard to resist.

CONCLUSION

This chapter has provided a sampling of the variety of intergenerational programs in existence. Every community has the resources needed to institute similar programs. The two most crucial elements are the youths and the older individuals who will constitute the volunteer corps. The examples of intergenerational programs in this chapter are suggestive of the opportunities awaiting these two groups. Professionals involved in the aging services network need to take the leadership role in bringing these generations together in service to each other and to their communities.

Chapter 3

Evaluation of Intergenerational Programs

Kenneth F. Backman
Kathleen Halberg

Evaluation is required and is an integral component of all successful programs, particularly intergenerational programs. As Rossi and Freeman (1993) state, evaluations are undertaken for a number of reasons: to assess the worth of ongoing programs; to estimate the usefulness of interventions to improve programs; to judge the utility of new and ongoing programs; to increase the effectiveness of a program's management or administration; and to satisfy accountability with program sponsors. It is likely as well that anyone involved in the administration or management of intergenerational programs realizes how essential evaluation is to the justification of budgets, personnel, and programming. Also a factor is the "political" process of obtaining next year's funding or any increase in funding.

Information derived from intergenerational program evaluations is required by groups such as: program decision makers, funding agencies, sponsoring institutions, advisory groups, community agencies, social service agencies that may be participants in the program, parents, and the public in general (Patton, 1990; Smink & Stank, 1992). All these groups, including the program staff, expect and desire the intergenerational program to be successful and evaluation is one of the ways program staff can provide that information. Researchers such as Krout (1993) and Henderson (1995) have suggested the following reasons for conducting an evaluation:

[Haworth co-indexing entry note]: "Evaluation of Intergenerational Programs." Backman, Kenneth F., and Kathleen Halberg. Co-published simultaneously in *Activities, Adaptation & Aging* (The Haworth Press, Inc.) Vol. 23, No. 1, 1998, pp. 27-33; and: *Preparing Participants for Intergenerational Interaction: Training for Success* (ed: Melissa O. Hawkins, Francis A. McGuire, and Kenneth F. Backman) The Haworth Press, Inc., 1999, pp. 27-33. Single or multiple copies of this article are available for a fee from The Haworth Document Delivery Service [1-800-342-9678, 9:00 a.m. - 5:00 p.m. (EST). E-mail address: getinfo@haworthpressinc.com].

- Assesses the intergenerational programs goals and objectives, and determines whether they are being met.
- Assesses the effectiveness of management and administration policies.
- Assesses any need for changes in the program.
- Monitors the program's implementation and performance.
- Improves in the delivery of services.
- Determines who is being served by the program.
- Identifies aspects of the program requiring adjustment.
- Provides information useful for long and short range planning.
- Assists in setting priorities and allocating resources.
- Determines the costs and benefits of components of the program.
- Assists in the assessment and training of staff and volunteers in the program.
- Provides program information for current and future funding sources.
- Provides an objective examination of intended and unintended program impacts.
- Develops staff skills and teamwork.
- Provides volunteers and staff with a sense of "ownership" and accomplishment, and an awareness of what can be done with the program.

Much time and planning must go into the evaluation of intergenerational programs. This chapter will outline the importance of systematic evaluation of intergenerational programs. Additional intergenerational program evaluation resources are provided at the end of this section.

Proper program evaluation has the potential to improve staff, justify funding, and provide credibility to the program. When planning a program evaluation, emphasis must be placed on the evaluation's feasibility (Halberg, 1995). Whether or not the program can actually be evaluated is a critical consideration. Defining specific program components to be evaluated may resolve this issue. For example, it may be possible to evaluate in terms of an increase in youth participants, however without extra work from program staff, it may be difficult to determine why participants drop out.

The evaluation process should not interfere with the program's mission. Therefore evaluation must be efficient (Halberg, 1995). For example, if the program staff do not have the skills required to conduct the program evaluation, outside sources need to be selected. Outside sources can include expert 'consultants' or a local university's faculty members familiar with evaluations and/or intergenerational programs. Selecting these outside evaluators at the onset of the intergenerational program will insure efficiency and provide a more comprehensive evaluation.

Types of Evaluation

As Smink and Stark (1992) and others suggest there are two basic areas required in intergenerational evaluation. There are two types of program evaluations needed to document the successes and weaknesses of intergenerational programs. They are formative or process evaluations and summative or outcome evaluations (Smink & Stank, 1992).

Formative or process evaluations focus on two major questions: (1) Is the program doing what was originally proposed or described? and (2) Is the project operating efficiently and in a timely manner? Summative or outcome evaluations address two primary questions as well. They are: (1) How well are the intergenerational program's goals and objectives being met? and (2) What effect is the program having on the participants in the program?

Halberg (1995) states that when addressing the formative evaluation questions, the efficiency with which the intergenerational program is being delivered is of primary importance. Determining the cost effectiveness of the program can be determined by calculating the cost of serving one participant in the program. Staff efficiency can be determined by calculating the number of participants served per unit of staff time (Halberg, 1995). Table 1 illustrates other issues involved in the formative evaluation including administrative matters like cost savings and determining reasons why volunteers, youth and staff drop out of the program.

The summative area of evaluation assesses what is happening to the participants during the intergenerational program (see Table 1 in Appendix). This can include their satisfaction with the program, the evaluation of the participants' attitudes regarding the program, and how the older adults feel about the youth and vice versa. Other related issues that may be evaluated are the morale or self-esteem of both the older adults and youth who are participating in the program. This assessment should occur both during the program and after the program has been discontinued (Halberg, 1995).

Evaluation Design and Execution

An issue to clarify when designing an intergenerational plan is why and for whom the evaluation is being done. Once these issues are addressed, the focus and the parameters of the evaluation design can be determined. Halberg (1995) suggests the following five questions to address in this process:

1. What is the purpose of the evaluation? Why is the evaluation plan being designed? For example, is the evaluation to be ongoing, quar-

terly or annually? Is it a special evaluation being done to justify next year's budget or the program's existence?

2. Who is requiring the evaluation? What is the audience for the evaluation report? Is it for the supervisor of the program, the staff, or the external funding source?

3. Are there any special concerns the evaluation audience may have regarding the program? If yes, what are they (e.g., will your audience be concerned primarily with cost effectiveness, participant satisfaction, or what)?

4. What will become of the evaluation once completed? (e.g., will the results remain internal to the program? Become part of a larger annual report? Become an asset of the project for the funder?)

5. What resources have been allocated to conduct the evaluation? What expertise is available (on staff or outside the program)? What administrative support and supplies are there on site and in the community?

Process of Intergenerational Evaluation

Every intergenerational evaluation plan will need to be adapted to that specific program. However, all plans will include general steps in the evaluation process. The following six phases of an evaluation process are adapted from Smink and Stank (1992):

Phase 1. Identify the components of the program to be evaluated, the specific program elements, procedures and/or activities.

Phase 2. Develop evaluation questions.

Phase 3. Select methods and procedures for data collection and analyses.

Phase 4. Operationalize evaluation questions (e.g., choose appropriate instruments and scales).

Phase 5. Collect data. Process, analyze, summarize and interpret findings.

Phase 6. Prepare the reports for the evaluation audiences.

In phase one of the evaluation process the program director or evaluation coordinator needs to review the program description, the program proposal and all other materials. The outcome of an analysis of the program goals and objectives should be a list of elements within the program that will require evaluation (Herman, Lyons-Morris, & Fritz-Gibbon, 1987; Smink & Stank, 1992).

The second phase, generation of evaluation questions, helps set the limits for the evaluation process by defining the depth and scope of information required by the audience for the evaluation. These evaluation questions need to assess the program's operation, and provide information on efficiency and effectiveness of the program (Smink & Stank, 1992). According to Herman et al. (1987) general questions that sponsors may have are: (1) What in the program needs attention? and Where is the program failing the youth or the older adults? Questions the evaluator may have are: (1) What is the goal of the intergenerational program? (2) Is the group in agreement about the program's goals? (3) Are these program goals being met? (4) Where is the program succeeding in achievement of its goals? and (5) Where is the program failing to achieve its goals?

With specific regard to formative evaluation, questions of sponsors may be: (1) How can the intergenerational program be improved? and (2) How can this intergenerational program become more efficient and effective? Questions the evaluator may have include: (1) What are the intergenerational program's most important characteristics–staff, volunteers, youth, activities location? (2) Are the intergenerational program's important characteristics being implemented? (3) What adjustments in the intergenerational program's management and support are required? and (4) What problems are there with the intergenerational program and how can they be solved? (Adapted from Herman et al., 1987).

Finally, some examples of questions the sponsor may have related to Summative Evaluation type assessment (adapted from Herman et al., 1987) are: (1) Is this intergenerational program worth continuing or expanding? (2) How effective is this intergenerational program? and (3) What does this intergenerational program look like and what does it accomplish? Questions the evaluator may have include: (1) Did the intergenerational program as planned occur? (2) What programs are available as alternatives to this intergenerational program? (3) How effective is this intergenerational program in comparison to other intergenerational programs? (4) How costly is this intergenerational program?

In phase three of the evaluation process, designs for data collection are directly related to the evaluation questions developed in phase two of the evaluation process. The data gathering method chosen will specify how and in what form the data will be collected. A few of the possible methods that could be utilized in the evaluation of intergenerational programs as presented by Halberg (1995) and Smink and Stank (1992) are:

- application forms
- existing published surveys/inventories
- pretest–posttest designs
- personal interviews
- focus groups
- self-administered questionnaires
- observation–formal and informal
- group dynamics process
- standardized tests and measures

Whichever one of the designs or combination of designs is used, care must be taken to ensure objectivity, reliability and validity of the information gathered. When in doubt, consult any of hundreds of research methods books in print or consult someone at a local university.

Phase four of the evaluation process occurs in conjunction with the third phase, and involves determining which data collection instruments will be used in the information gathering phase. Determining which instrument to use can be accomplished by reviewing the assessment tools used by other intergenerational programs, checking research on other social programs, or research methods texts. A local college or university library will also provide many scales for measuring such attitudes and opinions, self-esteem, achievement and many other issues important to the evaluation of intergenerational programs.

The data collection, analysis and interpretation in phase five of the evaluation process depends on the predetermined time schedule of data collection as stated in the original proposal of the program. It is very helpful if the data collection methods and instruments used are chosen and obtained either prior to the program beginning or at least two months prior to the actual collection of the data. Again, assistance with analysis and interpretation of the evaluation results can be found with faculty at your local university, if not available elsewhere in the program staff.

The final phase in the evaluation process is the production of the written report of the findings for the identified audience. This could be the decision-makers, funding agency or general public. This evaluation report should be organized around the selected evaluation questions and should contain some, if not all of the following sections (Smink & Stank, 1992):

1. A brief description of the intergenerational program and the program's goals and objectives as set out in the original proposal.
2. All of the selected evaluation questions related to the intergenerational program (e.g., needs assessment, formative or summative).
3. Components of the evaluation:

- a description of the design used;
- a description of the data collection method used for each group (older adult, youth, staff) including the instruments used, analysis completed and why this method was used;
- a summary of the data including graphical and numerical display of these results with appropriate interpretation provided;
- a summary of the overall results.
4. An executive summary of the intergenerational evaluation report for independent distribution.

Evaluation in intergenerational programs' as in all programs' should be an ongoing part of their operation. This evaluation process, just as the program as a whole, requires monitoring and revision on a regular basis (Halberg, 1995). The frequency of this revision will be dependent on the nature of the individual intergenerational program.

CONCLUSIONS

While space limits the depth with which the evaluation of intergenerational programs could be discussed, it is imperative to remember that all programs must include an evaluation component. While it would be naive to believe all programs have the expertise, resources, or time to do in-depth statistical types of evaluation, it is essential for all intergenerational programs to conduct some form of program assessment. Intergenerational programs have the potential to positively impact the lives of some of society's most deserving people. Evaluation can provide insight into the impact of an intergenerational program on its participants as well as the effectiveness and efficiency with which the program has in meeting its goals, and the goals of its sponsoring agencies.

Chapter 4

Community Awareness

Nancy Lindroth
Melissa O. Hawkins

INTRODUCTION

Chapters four and five are Community Awareness, which lacks great detail because of the consideration given to the varying community types, and Oral History, which provides the trainer with extensive information and resources on the topic.

Learning Objectives

1. Discuss the importance of learning about one's community.

Everyone can be an important, contributing member of his/her community. By learning about the community in which one lives, an individual can discover the resources of the community, as well as the best way to use them. It is the responsibility of the instructor to do extensive research on the community in order to convey valuable information. This research can take place at libraries, Chambers of Commerce, or through discussions with elders in the community.

2. Discuss how, when, why and by whom the community in question was formed.

[Haworth co-indexing entry note]: "Community Awareness." Lindroth, Nancy, and Melissa O. Hawkins. Co-published simultaneously in *Activities, Adaptation & Aging* (The Haworth Press, Inc.) Vol. 23, No. 1, 1998, pp. 35-38; and: *Preparing Participants for Intergenerational Interaction: Training for Success* (ed: Melissa O. Hawkins, Francis A. McGuire, and Kenneth F. Backman) The Haworth Press, Inc., 1999, pp. 35-38. Single or multiple copies of this article are available for a fee from The Haworth Document Delivery Service [1-800-342-9678, 9:00 a.m. - 5:00 p.m. (EST). E-mail address: getinfo@haworthpressinc.com].

35

Historical information can be gathered from the sources listed later in the chapter. Information about customs, on-going community activities such as festivals, and employment and recreational opportunities should be discussed.

3. Discuss and uncover the existing and potential roles held by participants in their community.

Roles held in the professional lives of people can aid them with volunteer activity in their community. Their experiences, associations, and colleagues can be great resources for a volunteer project, whether they are retired or not. There are numerous other roles individuals can play in their communities both formally and informally. These can be discovered through discussions with community natives, program participants, and leaders in the community.

4. Develop communication skills among all participants, regardless of their degree of familiarity with the community.

This can be accomplished by group sharing about communities in which they have lived.

INTRODUCTION: COMMUNITY AWARENESS

A training unit in Community Awareness is necessary to inform program participants about the community in which they live and operate their project. In the Howe-To Industries project, people with varying amounts of knowledge about the community were involved. Since the success of Howe-To Industries depended greatly upon community members, it was important for project participants to develop an understanding about the community and its inhabitants. Additionally, a training unit in Community Awareness is necessary to encourage loyalty and dedication.

Since all communities vary, an extensive description of the Howe-To Industries Community Awareness unit will not be provided. However, we have provided the broad subject areas and learning objectives needed to conduct a Community Awareness training unit.

COMMUNITY AWARENESS

Supplemental Information for the Instructor

Resources

- Local Chambers of Commerce
- Local Main Street Program

- County Economic Development Boards
- Municipal and County Planners
- Local Government or Councils of Government
- Tourism Agencies
- Local Visitors Center
- Local Historical Society

Find Answers to the Following Questions About Your Community

- Who spends time in this community?
    - Long-time residents
    - Transients (such as local military base personnel)
    - Part-time residents (such as seasonal residents in lake, shore or resort communities)
    - Young professionals, with or without children
    - Artists, college students, musicians, craftsmen
    - Tourists
    - Visitors looking to relocate or retire
    - New retirees
    - Corporations
    - What is the geography of this community? Geography played an important part in the settlement of the United States.
    - What was the impact of the lay of the land on the settlement pattern of this region? What impact does the geography of this region have on the community today?
    - What is the legal status of this community, and what is its political base? (e.g., Is it a place, community, town, borough, city, county, parish, or township?)
    - What are the demographics of this community?
    - What are the characteristics of its residents: race, sex, age, education, distance to work?
    - Who are the major employers in this community?
    - Industry (manufacturing, mining, agriculture, etc.)
    - Service
    - Government (state and federal)
    - Commercial and retail
    - Health care
- What factors affect the employment opportunities here?
    - Tourism
    - Retirement
    - Weather, climate or seasons

- Military and government installations, contractors, politics and budgets
- What does a newcomer need to know to settle in?
  - Utilities, local laws, drivers' licenses, etc.
  - Tax structure
  - Education opportunities
  - Higher learning opportunities
  - Cultural opportunities
- Where do residents and visitors spend their free time?
  - Recreational opportunities; federal, state, county, municipal, school, private, commercial
- Where are the community facilities?

  Cultural, meetings, voting, fire/police departments, hospitals, etc.
- What are the business resources available?
  - Non-profit
  - Financial institutions
  - Local and state government
  - Technical assistance
  - Financial assistance, other

- What hospitality resources are available to residents and visitors?
- What can you tell the visitor, in one page, about the community resources, activities and attractions?

- Distribute brochures on available activities
- Dining and lodging opportunities

Where can you find more information?

Chapter 5

Oral History

Robert B. Tietze
Steven L. Tunick

Learning Objective	Key Concepts/Terms	Instructor Notes
1. Define oral history.	generations; continuity; intergenerational	
2. Discuss the intergenerational nature of oral history projects.	intergenerational	
3. Discuss the initial phases of an intergenerational oral history project.	planning team goals and objectives; participant preparation	Exercise 1, Handout A, Handout B
4. Discuss the preparation necessary to be an oral history interviewer or interviewee.	interviewer; interviewee open-ended questions; leading questions	Exercise 2, Handout C Handout D, Handout E Handout F, Exercise 3
5. Discuss the interviewer/ interviewee relationship.	perspectives; flow of interview; roles	Exercise 4 Handout G
6. Discuss the method of conducting the oral history interview.	role playing; fluid and comfortable interview; active listening	Handout D Handout E

[Haworth co-indexing entry note]: "Oral History." Tietze, Robert B., and Steven L. Tunick. Co-published simultaneously in *Activities, Adaptation & Aging* (The Haworth Press, Inc.) Vol. 23, No. 1, 1998, pp. 39-59; and: *Preparing Participants for Intergenerational Interaction: Training for Success* (ed: Melissa O. Hawkins, Francis A. McGuire, and Kenneth F. Backman) The Haworth Press, Inc., 1999, pp. 39-59. Single or multiple copies of this article are available for a fee from The Haworth Document Delivery Service [1-800-342-9678, 9:00 a.m. - 5:00 p.m. (EST). E-mail address: getinfo@haworthpressinc.com].

Learning Objective	Key Concepts/Terms	Instructor Notes
7. Suggest the differences of intergenerational oral history projects.	promoting intergenerational relationships; stimulate thinking and discussion	Handout B
8. Discuss the proper way to conclude the oral history training session.		
9. Summarize key points.		Transparencies 1,2

INTRODUCTION: ORAL HISTORY

The trainer should begin with an introduction of him/herself and discuss the importance of an oral history project to a community. Participants should be made aware of the importance of preserving history for future generations. History allows the past to be revealed in such a way that communities can grow in a positive way, leaving behind past mistakes, and savoring past successes.

A great deal of time and energy can be saved by proceeding slowly during the early stages of the program. Brainstorming can create a great deal of excitement and enthusiasm and can generate many different activity ideas. This excitement is essential to the long term success of the program. It is especially important to inspire a genuine willingness in the participants to learn the interviewing techniques. In addition, the people being interviewed should become enthusiastic about sharing their past experiences with the interviewers. However, if the program is to truly succeed, it must be planned carefully. Each idea needs to be thoroughly explored before moving ahead. The most effective way to determine how to structure the oral history program is to create a team of people who have experience and knowledge within the community and who are interested in committing their time, energy and expertise.

IMPLEMENTATION AND MATERIALS SUGGESTIONS FOR THE INSTRUCTOR

This training session is ideally suited for no more than 40 participants. Seating can be arranged in any informal manner that encourages group discussion, and should be designed so that it is simple for participants to break into smaller groups when required. Oral history interviews will take place, with several youth interviewing an adult. Desks are probably not needed, as this is a discussion-oriented session. However, comfortable seating should be provided. This training session can last from between eight to sixteen hours, depending on the depth of discussions and interviews.

Supplies and Materials

Some things that you will or may need to conduct this training session include:

- overhead projector
- transparency markers
- extra transparencies, to make notes from the discussion for viewing purposes
- copier (to make copies of handouts)
- flip chart or chalk board (with markers or chalk)
- tape recorder and blank tapes

ORAL HISTORY

What Is Oral History?

Oral history is the gathering and preserving of historical information in spoken form. Through this process, oral history embodies the intergenerational ideal. By recording individuals' recollections of the past for use in the future, the wisdom and experience of older generations are shared with younger generations for the benefit of everyone. The oral history process provides an opportunity for young and old to gain new insights about themselves and one another. Oral history projects insure the continuity of one's people and one's traditions. Bringing individuals from different backgrounds together to explore the past can foster cross-cultural understanding and strengthen communities.

Oral History Projects Are Intergenerational in Nature

Community oral history projects are, in and of themselves, intergenerational in nature. They provide a bridge which connects the past to the present and enables both generations to begin to explore and understand how they have arrived where they are today. Sharing personal recollections with younger generations creates a conduit for elders to share their experiences, while adding new perspectives on important events in history. Sharing their lives in this way, elders once again play the vital role of guiding younger generations; a role which has been greatly diminished in our society. These experiences help younger people to make sense of their world. This perspective is important for young people exploring their own roles as emerging adults.

Initial Phases of an Intergenerational Oral History Project: Creating a Planning Team; Developing Clear Goals and Objectives; and Preparing Program Participants

The initial planning phase of an intergenerational oral history project should include the creation of a planning team, the development of clear goals and objectives, and the preparation of program participants. *Exercise 1* can help participants understand their own reasons for starting an oral history project. The instructor may wish to initiate this exercise just prior to the preparation of participants and after the explanation of the development of clear goals and objectives. *Handouts B, C, D, E and F* should also be used with this material.

Creating a Planning Team

More than one person is required to ensure that a project or program will be successful and continue to evolve and grow and develop its own legacy. For this reason, it is always a good idea to form a planning or advisory team to help generate ideas and create a plan for implementation. This team should bring together the skills, experience, and the contacts that will be needed to build a strong program. Also, it not only relieves one person of doing all of the work, but establishes a support structure and strong representation within the community. This sense of ownership should be one of the goals, as it will make the program measurably better. It is important that the advisory team be large enough to ensure a diversity of ideas and experience, but small enough to make decisions easily and put ideas into action.

To determine who should be involved in the initial planning process, the following factors should be considered:

1. Each of the collaborating agencies should be represented. In other words, if you represent a school and you want to develop an oral his-

tory program with a local senior center, and a local nursing home, someone from each organization will need to be included in the planning.

2. Support agencies should also be represented—Almost any oral history program can benefit from the resources offered by the local Historical Society, museums, and library. The local municipal office
may also be able to assist with important historical information
about the community and possibly help to identify older adults in
the community who can provide excellent "eye-witness" accounts
of historical events which affected the community.

The important thing to keep in mind is that the creation of these partnerships will make the program stronger and more effective. This also means
the dispersion of control to some degree. The original vision of the program may change somewhat as the program begins to reflect the diverse
ideas generated by the planning team.

Developing Clear Goals and Objectives

Developing goals and objectives is made much easier when a main goal
has already been stated in the beginning of the session. The goal, "To
design and implement a community intergenerational oral history project," is a viable goal for an oral history project. It is important to state this
goal clearly and arrive at consensus among the Planning Team, so that
everyone has the same vision.

The following is a sample of a program goal and its objectives:

> To create an interactive intergenerational oral history project to in-
> crease awareness and appreciation of our community's history.

The objectives will outline specifically how the goal will be achieved.
Here is a sample list of program objectives:

1. Prepare 30 students to conduct oral history interviews with selected
   community elders;
2. Transcribe oral history interviews for compilation into a publication
   made available to the community and available at the local library;
3. Establish a mini-museum at the local library for display and presentation of community artifacts, etc., and performances by storytellers,
   local poets, etc.
4. Provide regular get-togethers for both interviewers and interviewees
   at the local high school, or library, etc.
5. Share oral histories of community elders with elementary students.

Notice that the above are concise and brief. By keeping the goals and objectives simple, the likelihood of success is increased.

After the goals and objectives of the program have been agreed upon, it needs to be determined how those objectives will be achieved. This is a crucial point for the team because each person will need to determine which and how much of his/her resources he/she can reasonably commit. If the oral history project is taking place in a school setting, it is important to keep in mind that participants may have other duties to attend to. It must be made possible for the oral history program to be integrated into each person's schedule in order to appropriately serve everyone's commitments. When a program can be integrated into the schedule it is easier to make commitments of staff, time, and resources.

It may be a good idea to include the issue of commitment at the first planning team meeting. *Exercise 1* describes an effective way for each of the members of the new team to get to know one another and to learn about their partners.

Preparing Program Participants

Often, in the quest to get a project to the operation stage, we overlook some of the important skills and information which the participants will need. Preparing both the students and the older adults prior to getting started will help make the experience enjoyable, and can be designed into the program in order to establish a sense of excitement and fun. A series of well-planned workshops will help ease anxiety among the participants, give them a clear sense of the purpose and importance of the project, and ultimately make the project much more enjoyable. More importantly, this preparation will make the actual oral history interview more lively, meaningful, insightful and, ultimately, more informative.

In intergenerational oral history programs, the interviewers tend to be young people who interview older adults. To insure that these two generations establish trust and rapport, it is important to prepare both the interviewer and the interviewee. Regardless of whether the people interviewed are young or old, it is important to prepare them so that they feel comfortable sharing their history and therefore provide the best possible interview. *Exercise 2* describes the necessary preparation for an oral history interviewer.

The interviewer's preparation should include information about the following: Sensitivity to Aging, Introduction to Oral History, Topics to Discuss, and Communication Skills. *Exercise 3* describes the necessary preparation for the person being interviewed.

The interviewee's preparation should include the following themes:

The Importance of Sharing Details, Ways to Focus on Personal History, and Completing the Picture.

All of the activities described in *Exercises 2 and 3* underscore the need for both interviewer and interviewee to see themselves as a team working together to create a detailed snapshot of each other's lives. *Handout B* provides some examples of ideas for initiating oral history projects.

Discuss the Interviewer/Interviewee Relationship

An oral history project is a mutual process between both the interviewer and the interviewee. Therefore, it is important that the interviewees be as enthusiastic about the project as the interviewers. It is helpful if the interviewees enjoy talking about their lives, sharing their perspectives, and feel comfortable. Likewise, the interviewers should enjoy talking about the past and feel confident directing the flow of the interview.

Both the older adults and the youth should understand the goals of the program and their respective roles in its success. An example of preparation for an oral history program is a full-day workshop designed to bring local older residents identified by a senior center staff, with the youth who you plan to include in the oral history project. The workshop should be held at a school or a local establishment with easy access for both parties and should provide opportunities to introduce the groups to one another and develop skills necessary for the project.

It is important to identify ways in which young people and older adults can help one another, as well as reasons why a cooperative partnership is important to the community. When this had been achieved, the session participants are ready to look at a community Oral History program as a way to create this partnership. Participants are then able to engage in selected exercises from those listed in *Handout G. Exercise 4* describes a method to address issues related to Aging Sensitivity and Aging Stereotypes. An activity often serves as an ice-breaker as well as a method of focusing the group.

Conducting the Oral History Interview

There are several suggestions listed in *Handout D* for people who are going to conduct an oral history interview.

It can be very helpful for students to participate in role-playing exercises prior to conducting the actual interview. In preparation for the oral history project students can be paired and asked to interview one another.

During this exercise, the trainer should intervene to help focus the interview and develop methods for keeping the interview fluid and comfortable. The students learn how to listen actively to the interviewee. In this way, they are able to sense when the interviewee was more interested in the topic. By understanding these signals, they are able to adapt the interview to those points of interest. This fluidity is essential to a quality interview. Knowing when to move on to another question or topic and when to pursue new directions based on these signals from the interviewee is a learned art. The more practice the students have during the preparation stage, the better able they will be to conduct a skillful interview.

After they interview each other, the students can present their respective partner's history to the rest of the class. Students can also use these exercises to learn how to use the tape machines, how to introduce themselves, and how to conclude the interview and the visit.

Other areas covered during the preparation exercises include steps that must be undertaken in order to ensure a successful interview and are listed in *Handout E*. A signed release form should be obtained from the interviewee. This should be done after the interview and prior to leaving the interview site. In this way, if the interviewee feels uncomfortable about something, he/she has shared, they can decide not to allow the release of the interview.

Differences of Intergenerational Oral History Projects

When most people consider conducting oral histories, they envision one-on-one interviews where the interviewer has a list of prepared questions to be asked in a particular order and a tape recorder to record all responses for eventual transcription into written form. This method is commonly used and is an effective way to gather large quantities of information that might otherwise be lost. It is not always, however, the best way to promote intergenerational relationships or to stimulate thinking and discussion. There are a variety of innovative approaches which can be used to elicit stories while stimulating interaction and creativity. The program ideas listed in *Handout B* can be used as a springboard to create your own intergenerational oral history project. Additionally, *Handout G* may be helpful in providing fresh new ways of conducting an informative and fun oral history interview.

Concluding the Oral History Training Session

The session should be concluded with the youth giving a presentation to all of the other participants of the Oral History training session. The presentation should encompass what the youth learned about the older adults, as well as what they learned about their community. Any books, photographs, records, clothes, etc., should be used in this presentation in order to assist in describing the history of the community.

The older adults should also be asked what they have accomplished through participation in this program. Through the interviews, the older adults may have revived a memory that had long been gone, or they may have gained new knowledge into the history of the community.

Use *Transparencies 1* and *2* to summarize the material contained in this chapter upon completion of the session.

Oral History

Exercises, Handouts and Transparencies

Exercise 1: Getting to Know Each Other (Instructor Notes)

    a. Elders and youth who do not know each other should form small groups to discuss *Handout A.*
    b. After fifteen minutes, group discussion should take place.

Instructor should lead a group discussion around the suggestions described in *Handout A*. These questions are intended to give each team member an opportunity to better understand his/her partners.

HANDOUT A

1. Share your personal interest in oral history and why you believe it is important to the community.
2. Share a community myth that you know (example: "I remember the fire of . . . " or, "I remember Mrs. Jones, who lived on . . . ").

    This provides a small experiential exercise to help focus the group on its task.

3. Discuss how you can benefit by involvement in this new program.
4. Suggest a role that you may be able to play in making the program successful.

HANDOUT B

Ideas for initiating an intergenerational Oral History project:

Tracing Your Family's Roots

Most of us have a natural curiosity about our ancestry. Many of us have even traced our roots through traditional genealogical research. The oral history process adds depth and a human dimension to our family genealogical charts and migratory maps. Face to face interviews with our oldest living relatives and correspondence (in writing or on audio or videotape) with those family members who live at great distances allows our past to become part of our present reality. Their stories become our stories. Their struggles, their dreams and their accomplishments enrich our sense of self and give us a tangible connection to individuals and communities with whom we were previously unacquainted.

Discovering Your Community's History

An exciting cooperative venture for people of all ages is a compilation of their community's history. Who are its oldest citizens? What are their recollections of life in the neighborhood twenty, forty, sixty, or even eighty years ago? Has the topography changed? Have the same ethnic and religious groups always lived in the community? How have community residents reacted to changes in their world? What values have set the tone for life in the community? Including the memories of people from different ethnic and religious backgrounds in a community oral history project can be a wonderful way to enhance intercultural dialogue and to strengthen a community as a whole. Such projects can be especially helpful to institutions that are interested in enhancing their presence in a community or that are involved in community outreach.

Exploring Your Institution's Past

If your school, church, synagogue, club, library, or other organization is over twenty years old, an institutional history project can be of enormous benefit to persons of every generation. Persons of all ages who have been a part of the institution for a significant portion of their lives will have the opportunity to explore what the institution has meant to them over time and to be publicly recognized for their contributions. New members and children will feel a greater connection and commitment to the life of the institution. Finally, this exploration will turn naturally to a careful look at the present state of the institution and prompt an investment by all its members in shaping its future direction. Very often institutional oral histories are conducted in conjunction with significant turning points, such as special anniversaries or the dedication of a new wing.

Gaining Insight Into a Specific Topic Area

Oral histories are often utilized as a tool to explore the development of a particular idea or to enable participants to understand contemporary trends in a more personal way. For example, an exploration of the changing roles of women in society and in your specific community is greatly enhanced when the wisdom and experience of women of all ages are heard. Very often unexpected perspectives emerge that might not surface in an age-segregated group. Other examples of topical histories include the evolution of the family, immigrant experiences, work and school, and the role of religion in society. There are many different types of oral history projects in which your group could become involved. It is extremely important to take the specific nature and circumstances of your group into consideration when choosing what approach to take.

Exercise 2: Interviewer Preparation (Instructor Notes)

a. The group of people preparing to be interviewers should sit in a circle to discuss the topics on *Handout C*. A flip chart or chalk board may be used to write out the group's answers and encourage more discussion.
b. Mock interviews should be conducted, which emphasize communication skills and the "types" of questions. Group members should be paired, with the concentration only on interviewing skills. Exercise 3 explains the preparation for the interviewee.

Outlined in *Handout C* are the topic areas to be discussed among people preparing to be Oral History Interviewers. The Instructor will have to have knowledge of these areas and may wish to consult the resource list at the end of this chapter. Some additional matters to consider in preparation for an oral history interview can be found in *Handouts D* and *E*.

HANDOUT C

The following information is used to help one prepare to be an Oral History Interviewer. It is an outline of topic areas that will aid you in being a better interviewer of older adults.

1. Sensitivity to Aging

- What preconceptions do we share about the aging process and the elderly?
- Where did these ideas originate?
- Do these ideas and images tend to be largely positive or negative?

The Truth About Aging:

- psycho-social changes
- biological changes
- profile of the elderly in our community (numbers, where they live, institutions serving them, etc.)

The next part of this volume will contain a chapter on *Aging Sensitivity,* which will to help with your understanding of older age groups.

2. Introduction to Oral History

- What is history?
- How do events get recorded?
- Can/should history be an objective account?
- What can we learn from interviewing elders?

3. Topics to Discuss

Compose a list of topic areas and general questions to cover. This list should be an outline, not the actual questions that the interviewers ask. Interviewers should conduct some preliminary research. This may include: creating a family tree, developing a community map, reading published oral histories on specific topics.

4. Communication Skills

Interviewers should be conscious of their enunciation, tone of voice, and body language.
   a. enunciation–pronouncing each syllable of a word by uttering articulate sounds
   b. tone of voice–the pitch and vibration in one's manner of speaking
   c. body language–the manner in which one uses his/her body when communicating

Remember to use who, what, when, where, and how questions, open-ended questions, and follow-up questions.

HANDOUT D

The following information is helpful for persons preparing to do an oral history interview.

1. Before the Interview

- Learn all you can about the subject you are researching by reading available written sources and by talking casually with informed people.
- Develop a list of suggested interview topics with possible subtopics under each topic. Don't phrase these as questions–to do so might inhibit the flexibility required in an interview.
- Develop a file of potential interviewees. It is impossible to determine what makes a "good" interviewee, but keep in mind the following criteria: a willingness to talk candidly and for the record; a certain reflectiveness about one's experience; a keen eye for details–and an ability to remember them; and an interest in remembering the past. Also, it is very important to choose people with a variety of different perspectives on your subject.
- Once you have decided on a person to interview, contact her/him about the possibility of an interview. Explain your project, the uses to which the taped interview will be put, and the value of his/her participation. Go over what topics you plan to cover.
- Prepare an interview outline for yourself. This is not a list of "20 Questions," but an outline of the topics you want to interview the person about. You will very likely stray from your outline in the actual interview, but hopefully, your outline will serve as a general guide.
- Set up a time and a place for your interview session. Allow about two hours for an interview session; though you may not be taping the whole time, you will need time to set up and then leave gracefully. Pick a place that is convenient and comfortable and has few distractions.
- Be familiar and comfortable with your recording equipment. Practice using the controls.
- Bring to the interview an extension cord, at least two times as many cassettes as you'll need, a small notebook, and a release form indi-

cating the interviewees' knowledge that the session is being re-corded.
- Put an introduction on the tape before you go to the interview, in-cluding your name, the name of your interviewee, the subject of the interview, the place of the interview, and the date.

(Source: Linda Shopes, Pennsylvania Historical & Museum Commission.)

HANDOUT E

The following is a guide to aid Oral History interviewers.

- Arrive on time.
- The key to a good interview is the rapport you as the interviewer es-tablish with your interviewee. Your job is to create a relaxed, expan-sive atmosphere so that your interviewee will want to share his/her life experiences with you in an open, honest manner.
- After recording for a couple of minutes, stop the machine and play back what you have done. This allows the interviewee to breathe again and allows you to check on the quality of your work. After this, however, it is best to call as little attention to the tape recorder as possible during the interview.
- Let your interviewee do most of the talking. Function simply as a guide by asking brief, clearly-stated, open-ended questions. Avoid leading questions ("Don't you think that . . . ") and questions that yield yes or no answers. Don't interrupt; use your notepad to jot down follow-up questions as they come up so that you can ask them later.
- Let your interviewee finish one general topic before jumping on to the next. Use follow-up questions to probe for more information, greater detail, more contextual data, values and feelings.
- Strike a balance between following your planned interview outline and following leads your interviewee opens up to you during the ses-sion. Be flexible.
- Start with more impersonal areas of questioning and then move into more sensitive areas as the interview progresses. People reveal them-selves slowly. Try to get your interviewee to stick to his/her own per-sonal experience, rather than speak in generalities.
- Don't avoid sensitive or controversial subjects. Try to get the whole story, not just the positive side. If an interviewee seems to be pre-

senting a very distorted account, you might simply state that other sources you have consulted take an opposing view and then see what the interviewee's reaction is.

- Try to finish in an hour and a half. If an interview has gone on for this length and still is incomplete, set up another appointment and continue at a later date.
- After completing the actual taping, don't leave abruptly. Give your interviewee some time to relax. You may have stirred up powerful memories.
- Before you leave, make sure the interviewee signs a release form. She/he should know in advance about the release form.
- Ask your interviewee if she/he knows of any photographs, material objects or written records that might be useful to your project.

Exercise 3: Interviewee Preparation (Instructor Notes)

Exercise 3 is broken into three activities: The Importance of Sharing Details, Ways to Focus on Personal History, and Completing the Picture. These activities can be found on *Handout F.*

The group of people preparing to be interviewees should be broken down into groups of three or four. Each person in the group should go through each activity, sharing with the rest of the members of the small group.

a. For the activity, "Completing the Picture," pairs should be formed.
b. After the three activities, the group should come back together to discuss experiences, questions, etc.

The Instructor should circulate to each small group to make sure everyone is receiving time to participate equally. For the activity, "The Importance of Sharing Details," the Instructor should guide participants based on the questions on the handout they will receive.

A ten minute break should be given after the activity, "Ways to focus on Personal History." When everyone returns, group members should pair up for "Completing the Picture." Finally, the entire group should come back together to discuss the activities in which they were involved.

HANDOUT F

The following information will give you helpful tips in being a more attentive and cooperative person in an Oral History interview. Within your small group, carry out the activities outlined below. For the final activity, you will be in groups of two.

1. The Importance of Sharing Details

Often people need help in recognizing important pieces of "information" in their lives. Here is just one suggested activity for helping interviewees sharpen their eye for detail:

> Close your eyes and imagine the house in which you grew up. Focus on sharp details (e.g., "let's start in the kitchen . . . "). Continue to "walk" through your childhood home answering questions such as: What were some of the most memorable events which took place there? Which room was your favorite? Which room was your least favorite? Was there a time when all the lights went out and what did you do? Share your memories with your small group.

2. Ways to Focus on Personal History

A fun way to begin sharing personal histories is to focus on your own name. Questions you can ask each other include:

- Who were you named for?
- What do you know about this person?
- Have you ever had any nicknames?
- What does your name mean?
- Based on some of your life experiences, what would you like your name to mean?
- Have you ever wanted to change your name?
- What name would you choose?

3. Completing the Picture

Responding to the interviewer's questions beyond one or two sentences is often difficult. Here is a 3-stage activity to help interviewees "complete the picture" and enhance the interview: (a) One person should ask the other a "yes" or "no" questions such as, "Do you or have you ever had any pets?" (b) The interviewee must talk continuously for at least 3 minutes without further questioning. (c) After the three minute period, the interviewer should ask follow-up questions.

HANDOUT G

These are exercises designed to enhance the relationship between the interviewer and the person who is being interviewed, specifically younger people and older adults.

1. Music Across Ages

Explore each decade of this century using popular music to underscore general trends or to focus on specific issues (e.g., women's roles, religion, romance). Encourage sing-alongs where appropriate. Culminate with an intergenerational "Name That Tune" game.

Record short phrases from popular songs from the 1920's to the present on a cassette tape. Mix the decade and song styles so no one will have any idea of what is coming next. Intergenerational teams of four to six players each should take turns guessing the tune. You'll be surprised at how many of the old favorites are familiar to the youth and how many older adults recognize contemporary pop hits.

2. Rap Writing

An exciting way to make stories come alive is to turn them into rap songs. Raps are simple to create and the composers can range in age from elementary school children to older adults. Young people can write raps about older adults or young and old can compose raps together about common themes.

3. Recipe Sharing

In this age of fast food and microwaves, many cultural traditions involving cooking, old family recipes and shared meals are becoming only a memory. Bringing young and old together to prepare Christmas cookies, matzo ball soup or homemade ravioli is an activity that is fun and involves active participation by all. It is a wonderful way for informal story telling to take place. Your group might consider publishing a cookbook that not only includes recipes but also the cultural and personal traditions surrounding them.

4. Community Map

Robert Venturi designed a small park in a historic area of Philadelphia. The park is paved with slate and granite to represent the original grid pattern of the city in miniature. Trees are planted where parks are located. Surrounding the park is information on William Penn, the city's founder. Groups engaged in a study of their community's history can replicate this type of community map using butcher paper in place of granite. Replicas of houses, parks and public institutions can be included and "Walking Tours of the Neighborhood" can be conducted.

5. Photograph Exchanges

A fun way to explore social history and to teach observation skills to children is through the sharing of old photographs. Photographs not only capture individuals and families at a particular moment in history but also capture styles of dress, interior design, economic status and family relations.

6. Treasured Objects

An adapted "show and tell" program is a great springboard for discussions of personal and family history. Ask each participant to bring in an object that holds personal meaning for them and their family. Old rolling pins, antique jewelry from great grandmother, ritual candlesticks and porcelain dolls are but a few of the objects commonly shared. These objects encourage reminiscing about the past and can stimulate discussion about why we value objects of the past and what they represent for us. Ask an historian to join the group for this session. She/he may be able to unlock mysteries about the origins of specific objects and paint a richer picture of the era of the object's origin.

7. Fashion Show

It is amazing how many people save clothing from past eras in the back of their closets or in a trunk in the attic. Collect the old dresses, shoes, hats, etc., and stage a fashion show of the attire of each decade. Supplement the clothing with songs, dances and photographic slides of each era. You may want to add an extra intergenerational component by dressing the young people in clothing from the past and the older adults in contemporary fashions.

8. Living in the Past

If your group is experiencing an important anniversary, celebrate it by transporting yourselves for one day to that significant year. For example, if the year of your group's founding was 1925, encourage everyone to wear clothing either original to that time or to wear replicas of clothing from that time. Find recordings of old radio shows, screen an old silent movie, and distribute copies of old newspapers. Conduct a group meeting as if it were actually taking place in that year and put topics on the agenda relevant to that era.

9. Wisdom School

Your group may be blessed with a small number of truly extraordinary older adults. If this is the case, you may want to sponsor a "Wisdom School." Invite four to six remarkable elders to (make presentations to a mixed age audience in a panel discussion format). Ask them to reminisce about life experiences that shaped them and encourage them to offer their wisdom to the assembled.

10. Treasure Hunt

A particularly effective way to engage younger children in an oral history project is to design a treasure hunt. Teens, middle-age persons and older adults together can create the format, developing clues that will lead the participants to people with interesting stories, archival records and artifacts.

11. Station to Station

Another program for young children, similar to the Treasure Hunt but easier to execute, involves small groups of children traveling from one older adult to another. At each station (either in separate rooms or spread out in the social hall), an older adult tells an interesting story about her/his early life. Encourage the adults to include "props" with their presentations. They might wear an outfit from their youth, display old photographs, pass around treasured objects or even distribute homemade chocolate chip cookies (made from an old family recipe, of course).

12. Time Capsules

A new twist on always popular time capsule activities is for intergenerational groups to develop time capsules representing past decades. Unlike a contemporary time capsule, there is no need to gather authentic artifacts. Old photographs can be reproduced and old objects can be replicated. One interesting approach is to involve a number of cross-age groups and ask each to choose a different decade. At the end, bring the time capsules together and see how similar or dissimilar they are. This will lead to a fruitful discussion on changes in value systems.

Exercise 4: Age Line (Instructor Notes)

    a. In this exercise, participants are asked to line up from oldest to youngest without speaking. Once in the line, ask participants to visualize their place in the continuum, in relation to the others. Then ask them to share the things that they like about being at that stage of life, as well as the things that they don't like about their age. As the group explores their feelings about being a particular age, give participants the opportunity to "change" their age by moving to a new place in the line. They can also place others at the point in line where they believe the others belong.

    b. Following the age-line activity (which serves to focus the group), the group should be broken down to work in small groups to identify age-related stereotypes within society. They should also examine their personal reactions to stereotypes when directed toward themselves.

The Instructor is required to facilitate this activity. Discussion should be encouraged, sharing the reasons why individuals have "chosen" a new age, as well as their impressions of other ages and age stereotypes. This exercise is a particularly good "ice-breaker," if used at the beginning of the training session.

Note: This exercise is also provided for use in the Aging Sensitivity chapter. It is left up to the instructor to decide where he or she would find the exercise to be most useful.

Transparency 1
Oral History

Key Points

1. What is <u>oral history?</u>

- The gathering and preserving of historical data in spoken form
- Stories
- Myths
- Local legends

2. Why is an oral history project <u>intergenerational</u> in nature?

- Provides a bridge between the past and the present, the old and the young.
- Gives older people a chance to share their experiences with the young; helps younger people see the world from a new perspective.

3. Oral history helps to <u>strengthen</u> <u>communities</u>.

Transparency 2
An Intergenerational Oral
History Project

The Initial Phases

1. Creating a Planning Team

- The team should bring together skill, experience and contacts with the necessary resources and people.
- Each of the agencies involved should be represented.
- Support agencies should also be represented (e.g., museums, libraries, etc.).
- A strong team can help ensure a great project!

2. Developing Goals and Objectives

- Clear goals and objectives should be outlined, to ensure that all involved parties have the same vision for the project.
- After goal and objective statements have been made, a plan for achieving each of them should be determined.

3. Participant Preparation

- Skill building-workshops, including interview/communication skills and sensitivity training, are a must.

Chapter 6

Introduction to Sensitivity

Karen Paisley

"Know your audience" is a mantra common to many fields, from business to recreation. The practice of designing goods and services that suit the demographics of a particular audience involves the fundamental realization that audiences are *different*. This further implies that the particular characteristics of a target population for a product or program should affect its design and presentation.

On a simplistic level, for example, it is likely that a strenuous rock climbing expedition would be more appropriate for adolescents than for seniors. By the same token, Big Band music would tend to be more appealing to seniors than to adolescents. However, there is an inherent flaw in these examples: Within the groups of seniors and adolescents, there are bound to be exceptions to the generalizations. Therefore, it is not enough to know your audience based on simple labels. In order to be truly effective, practitioners must come to view any audience as an amalgamation of heterogeneous individuals.

Beyond the basic knowledge of differences, as well as beyond the realm of political correctness, lies the construct of sensitivity. Sensitivity reaches past the acknowledgment of fundamental demographic differences between groups to a deeper concern for each group's needs and emotions. It is not sufficient to merely *know* that people differ at fundamental levels, such as age and ethnicity. Efforts should be made to understand, appreciate, and accommodate even the more subtle differences that occur between

[Haworth co-indexing entry note]: "Introduction to Sensitivity." Paisley, Karen. Co-published simultaneously in *Activities, Adaptation & Aging* (The Haworth Press, Inc.) Vol. 23, No. 2, 1998, pp. 69-73; and: *Preparing Participants for Intergenerational Interaction: Training for Success* (ed: Melissa O. Hawkins, Francis A. McGuire, and Kenneth F. Backman) The Haworth Press, Inc., 1999, pp. 61-65. Single or multiple copies of this article are available for a fee from The Haworth Document Delivery Service [1-800-342-9678, 9:00 a.m. - 5:00 p.m. (EST). E-mail address: getinfo@haworthpressinc.com].

and within each group. This introduction, then, seeks to document the current need for sensitivity.

THE CASE FOR SENSITIVITY

In a 1996 edition of *Reader's Digest*, the vocabulary quiz called "It Pays to Enrich Your Word Power" focused on words from the twenty-first century. These words, now part of Merriam-Webster's Collegiate Dictionary, Tenth Edition (1996), epitomized some of the dramatic changes that have occurred in recent years:

- ethnic cleansing–the act of expelling, imprisoning or killing ethnic or racial minorities by a dominant majority group
- maquiladora–foreign-owned factory in Mexico where imported parts are assembled in products for export
- mommy track–career path that allows a mother flexible or reduced work hours but tends to slow or block advancement
- telecommuter–someone who works at home using an electronic link to the office
- grunge–person who is untidy, shabby or obnoxious; also rock music incorporating elements of punk rock and heavy metal

These few examples serve to illustrate the extent to which society has changed as manifested by changes in vocabulary. Various age cohorts and ethnic groups perceive the world differently. These differences, when not addressed with sensitivity, can constitute gaps.

THE GENERATION GAP

The term "Generation Gap," according to anthropologist Margaret Mead (1978), is a proper noun that includes many smaller gaps. There are differences between old-school parents and modern children, urban and rural dwellers, immigrants and native-born family members, and staunchly religious individuals and those on a constant quest for meaning (p. xvii). Such gaps are the foundation for both growth and misunderstanding. The evolution of the Generation Gap is linked to the rate of change in a particular society and, more specifically, which generation has its finger on the pulse of this change. Mead (1978) classifies societies, based on the rate of change and its ramifications, as postfigurative, cofigurative, and prefigurative.

A postfigurative society is one in which the rate of change is so gradual that, in essence, the future is *no different* than the past (Mead, p. 13). As a result, most of the teaching is done by parents or other adults with children or younger adults as the pupils. Adults know the norms of the society's functioning and pass this knowledge on to the younger generations. Most cultures that fit this description are considered primitive by American standards since the level of technology, as we know it, is low. Extended families are common, and the youngest pattern themselves from the oldest.

In a cofigurative society, the present serves only as a *guide* for the future. Change is occurring quickly, so each generation is expected to differ from those in the past. Since this is the case, each generation tends to learn primarily from other members of the same generation. Society's norms are gradually changing, so individuals will model their behavior to that of their contemporaries rather than to previous generations (Mead, p. 39). While some learning is transferred from adult to child, much of the adult's knowledge will be obsolete by the time the child matures.

If the rate of change continues to increase, a society becomes prefigurative. In this case, the child becomes the adult's teacher. Technology and other new information is being introduced so quickly that children, in an educational mode and not burdened by work, are the first to learn. Not only is new information becoming available, but it tends to supersede previous knowledge. According to Steinberg (1996), "Instead of parents asking, 'Why can't Johnny read?' teenagers ask, 'Why can't Mom and Dad program the VCR?'" (p. 185).

Based on these definitions, the United States as a whole is clearly a cofigurative society. The dramatic changes in fashion, music, political attitudes, and other areas clearly indicate that previous generations are not simply recreated. Individuals identify most closely with other members of their own generation. For example, while teens do value their parents' opinions on matters affecting their future, they depend more heavily on peers for daily consultation (Steinberg, p. 342). With closer consideration, however, America can also be viewed as approaching the status of a prefigurative society. This is especially true with respect to technology, but applies in other areas as well. Today's teens are confronted with situations unlike those faced by any previous generation. According to Strasburger (1993):

> For baby boomers, the threat to world peace was omnipresent. Now the threats are closer to home. No previous generation of teenagers had to confront anything even remotely like HIV. No previous generation saw so many young people exposed to alcohol, cigarettes, pregnancy, sexually transmitted diseases, suicide and violence. (p. 57)

Thus, as recipients and keepers of the newest information, today's youths have become the teachers and the United States faces the Generation Gap from a new perspective.

While the United States may be classified as having a combination of cofigurative and prefigurative aspects, any real shift, such as that occurring after the industrial revolution, is irreversible (Mead, p. 66). Each generation takes on new roles as teacher or pupil as these shifts occur. The level of conflict surrounding the Generation Gap is based on how well each group adjusts to its relative position.

Returning to the issue of sensitivity, Steinberg (1996) refers to the notion of the "personal fable" when describing adolescents. This notion is based on the belief that one's experiences are truly unique and that no one else can possibly understand one's particular situation (p. 67). This view, however, is not solely characteristic of adolescents, as is illustrated by a senior's egocentric view of the way things used to be. Sensitivity requires that this outlook be shed by all parties, young and old alike. Whether or not the journey is "uphill both ways," each generation must attempt to walk in the others' shoes.

Racial and Ethnic Gaps

The egocentrism of the personal fable can be logically extrapolated to an ethnocentric view of the "cultural fable." This notion is based, then, on a culture's belief that its experiences are unique and that no other culture has endured or enjoyed the same circumstances. While this is, in fact, an undeniably justified stance for some ethnic groups, the practice of sensitivity calls for an appreciation of *all* cultures.

The United States is clearly made up of many different ethnic groups, each with their own culture, traditions, norms, and sense of identity. Additionally, each group has its own history of hardships and triumphs. The notion of sensitivity does not attempt to equalize or negate diversity, but rather seeks to harmonize and facilitate coexistence. A stance of cultural superiority, then, is directly incompatible with sensitivity and, once again, must be abandoned if any gaps are to be bridged.

In addition to the mere presence of many different ethnic and racial groups, shifts from minority to majority status are occurring for some of these groups in many areas of the country. Similar to generational shifts in roles as societies move from cofigurative to prefigurative, ethnic groups shifting to and from majority status will also need to assume new roles. Since it is inevitable that individuals from different racial and ethnic backgrounds will come in contact with each other, relations can only benefit from genuine attempts to understand the needs and emotions of each group.

Ethnic and racial sensitivity, like intergenerational sensitivity, is a conscious process requiring empathy and commitment. Additionally, sensitivity is a necessary requirement for any program involving a diverse group of people. The following chapters provide information designed to foster a more complete knowledge of at-risk youths, the aging population, and ethnic and racial diversity. It is hoped that this material will facilitate the transition from simply knowing an audience to being sensitive to individuals.

Chapter 7

Understanding and Mentoring with At-Risk Youths

Paul S. Wright

Learning Objective	Key Concepts/Terms	Instructor Notes
1. Discuss the characteristics of At-Risk Youths.	Violence; substance abuse; poverty; neglect; failure in school; low self-esteem; teen pregnancy; negative role models; truancy; physical abuse; delinquency	Exercise 1
2. Discuss warning signs that suggest an adolescent needs outside help.	Signs of suicide, drug or alcohol abuse, physical abuse. Warning signs; major weight loss; poor self-image; problems at school; depression; delinquency	Exercise 2 Handout A
3. Discuss Richard Jessor's Conceptual Framework for Adolescent Risk Behaviors.	Risk and Protective Factors; Risk Behaviors/Lifestyles; Risk Outcomes	Transparency 1
4. Discuss the context and development of adolescents.	Interaction of family, school and neighborhood in adolescence	
5. Discuss the definition and rationale behind mentoring.	Mentoring definition; rationale; contribution to adolescent growth	Exercise 3 Handout B
6. Discuss the roles of a mentor.	Educator; active listener; sharer; encourager; friend; role model	Exercise 3 Handout C

[Haworth co-indexing entry note]: "Understanding and Mentoring with At-Risk Youths." Wright, Paul S. Co-published simultaneously in *Activities, Adaptation & Aging* (The Haworth Press, Inc.) Vol. 23, No. 2, 1998, pp. 75-99; and: *Preparing Participants for Intergenerational Interaction: Training for Success* (ed: Melissa O. Hawkins, Francis A. McGuire, and Kenneth F. Backman) The Haworth Press, Inc., 1999, pp. 67-91. Single or multiple copies of this article are available for a fee from The Haworth Document Delivery Service [1-800-342-9678, 9:00 a.m. - 5:00 p.m. (EST). E-mail address: getinfo@haworthpressinc.com].

67

7. Discuss the three stages of the mentoring relationship.	Stage 1: Building trust; Stage 2: Reaching Goals; Stage 3: Terminating the Relationship	Handout D
8. Discuss the ideal characteristics of a mentor.	Be knowledgeable; don't judge; find the strengths; life skills instruction; advocacy support; active listening	Handout E
9. Discuss the relationship held between older adults and youths.	Lack of adequate social support structures; similarities between groups	
10. Summarize key points.		Transparency 2

INTRODUCTION: MENTORING WITH AT-RISK YOUTHS

The instructor should begin with an introduction of him/herself and discuss the importance of familiarizing the older participants with the issues involved in working with "at-risk" youths. It is also important for the instructor to stress the ideal attributes of a mentor. Mentoring can be a successful and rewarding venture for both parties if they enter the relationship with an awareness of each other's backgrounds and life circumstances.

Mentoring, as explained in the text of this chapter, is the relationship that results from pairing an older individual with a child or adolescent who is in need of some extra support or guidance. The mentor establishes regular contact with his or her mentee and becomes a non-judgmental, concerned, and active adult figure in that child's or adolescent's life.

Mentoring is a method often used in an effort to give help and guidance to "at-risk" youths. A child is considered at-risk if he/she is exposed to circumstances that may prevent him or her from achieving a productive adulthood. These circumstances are outlined in the text, and may include issues such as physical abuse and poverty.

Adolescents who are at-risk, or experiencing some of the circumstances that could place them at-risk, often behave in a manner that may be difficult for older people to understand. It is important for mentors to become aware of the things that at-risk youths are faced with, so that they can deal with their mentee more effectively. The job of a mentor requires patience, good interpersonal skills, and an understanding of the mentee's situation. It is the purpose of this session to help mentors recognize what challenges the youths of today are facing, so they can become better prepared for this rigorous, but rewarding, endeavor.

IMPLEMENTATION AND MATERIALS SUGGESTIONS
FOR THE INSTRUCTOR

This training session is ideally suited for 30 participants. Since it is a session geared toward older, volunteer mentors, the seating arrangements should be made as comfortable as possible. The seating should also be arranged in such a manner so as to encourage free discussion among participants and with the instructor. This session will last approximately two hours.

Supplies and Materials

Some things that you will or may need for this training session include:

- overhead projector
- transparency markers
- extra transparencies
- copier (to make copies from handouts)
- chart or chalk board (with markers or chalk)
- pencils for use with the handouts

MENTORING WITH AT-RISK YOUTHS

Characteristics of At-Risk Youths

In her nationally acclaimed book, *Adolescents At Risk*, Joy Dryfoos (1990) defined a child as at-risk if he/she is in danger of not achieving a productive adulthood. Furthermore she concluded that approximately 25% of all adolescents aged between 10 and 17 years of age are at serious risk of not achieving productive adulthood, with an additional 25% at moderate risk. Others conclude that all our nation's children are at-risk for one reason or another.

At-risk youths should be viewed as "potential achievers" who at any point in their lives are not performing at their level of potential. This is largely a direct result of a multitude of issues that they are experiencing in home, family, school, and community environments, and these issues are impacting negatively on their attitudes and behaviors. Some of these specific issues are briefly discussed below.

Violence–The portrayal of violence in vivid color and in graphic detail by the media has become so commonplace that a tolerance seems to have been developed. Adolescents are victimized by violent crime (rape, robbery and assault) at almost twice the rate of the general population. Moreover, the incidence of potentially life threatening violence has increased significantly over the course of the last few years.

Substance abuse–Alcohol, nicotine and marijuana have been the traditional substances abused by adolescents. However, a number of highly dangerous addictive drugs, such as heroin, cocaine, and "speed", have begun to find their way into schools and communities. Johnson (1990) reported that an astounding 60+% of all high school seniors had experimented with illicit drugs.

Physical abuse–Abuse by a child's or adolescent's parents, step-parents, siblings or others can lead to disturbing problems in that child's development. It can also lead to withdrawal or a general mistrust in people or adults.

Poverty–The single-most consistent indicator of youths at-risk is low household income. During early 1988, nearly one out of every five adolescents (ages 13 to 18) was a member of a family with a collective income well below the poverty line (Sum & Fogg, 1991). Poverty, compounded with a drastic reduction in caring, supportive families, places a significant majority of adolescents at-risk.

Failure in school–In the U.S. nearly one-third of all students drop out before completing high school. According to Milliken (1994), not only does every class of dropouts on average make $237 billion less than an equivalent class of high school graduates, but also 82% of all Americans in prison are high school drop-outs. Poor academic performance can also lead to low self-esteem and an increase in detrimental attention-seeking behavior.

Other issues–Other issues worthy of mention when looking at at-risk youths include the disturbing increase in the incidences of teen pregnancy, juvenile delinquency, vandalism, gang membership and peer pressure. Together with a decline in community and family support systems, society paints a grim picture for the developing adolescent.

Exercise 1 is designed to be used with this section.

Cries for Help

Usually there are a number of warning signs that suggest that an adolescent is having problems at home, at school or in their community. When an adult observes one or more of these "cries for help" in an adolescent he or she knows, it is often a sure indicator of trouble. Some of these warning signs are discussed below.

Suicide–Some signs that suggest a child might be considering suicide include: Giving away possessions, composing a will, constant talk about death and dying, prolonged depression, saying the family would be better off without him or her, evidence of a plan or method, and being suddenly at peace.

Drug or alcohol abuse–Warning signs include: Irrational or "spaced out" behavior, sudden increase in accidents, deceitfulness, loss of interest in school, secretiveness, severe mood swings, increase in time spent alone or sleeping, and the smell of alcohol on breath or on clothes.

Physical abuse–Abuse comes in a variety of different forms and can be received from a number of different people in a child's world. It might be sexual abuse, mental abuse, violence, neglect or incest. Some warning signs that a child is enduring a form of abuse might include: Non-accidental physical injury, frequent unexplainable accidents, withdrawal and depression, running away from home, and a sudden onset of compulsive and/or self-destructive behavior.

Other signs that might indicate a child's non-verbal cry for help include: Major weight loss, loss of appetite, poor self-image, dramatic decline in academic performance, serious depression, law-breaking behavior, eating disorders, hypochondria and an increase in risk-taking behaviors. *Exercise 2* and *Handout A* are to be used as teaching aids here.

Conceptual Framework for Risk Behavior

Dr. Richard Jessor (1992) developed a model which illustrated that in the lives of all adolescents there are certain "Risk" factors and certain "Protective" factors. This framework breaks risk-behavior into five broad classifications: Biology/Genetics, Social Environment, Perceived Environment, and Personality and Behavior. Protective factors are conceptualized as decreasing the likelihood of engaging in problem behavior through direct personal or social controls against its occurrence (e.g., strong religious commitment or predictable parental sanctions); through involvement in activities that tend to be incompatible with or are alternatives to problem behavior (e.g., activities with the family or with church groups); and through orientations toward and commitments to conventional institutions (e.g., schools) or to adult society more generally. In contrast, risk factors are conceptualized as increasing the likelihood of engaging in problem behavior through direct instigation or encouragement (e.g., failure or frustration instigating a coping response, or models and influence from peers); through increased vulnerability for normative transgression (e.g., low self-esteem); and through greater opportunity to engage in problem behavior (e.g., membership in an antisocial peer group) (Jessor, Van Den Bos, Vanderryn, Costaid, & Turbin, 1994). Though very little can be done to directly impact such risk factors as family history, poverty, parents and friends as models for deviant behavior, risk-taking propensity and poor academic performance, recreation professionals through quality pre-scriptive programming can positively reinforce protective factors. Factors such as high intelligence, neighborhood resources, effective role models, high self-esteem and community involvement are all factors which can be potentially enriched through recreation and leisure programs.

Jessor's model theorizes that the prevalence or lack of risk and protec-tive factors directly influences certain adolescent risk behaviors/lifestyles which, in turn, can result in undesirable risk outcomes. The merit of this model is in its ability to highlight the many environmental and contextual factors that contribute to adolescent behavior. Certainly a mentoring pro-gram cannot hope to reduce all risk factors and increase all protective factors, but mentoring programs are valuable initiatives in the facilitation of productive adulthood. *Transparency 1* provides a visual model of Jes-sor's theory.

Context and Development of Adolescents

Chronbach (1982) states that "understanding an adolescent's experi-ence . . . seems to require a community-wide ecological perspective . . . and the investigator will enrich his interpretation by acquainting himself with the context in which his limited unit is embedded." Adolescents are firmly embedded simultaneously in the three contexts of family, school and neighborhood, and each has a unique and considerable impact on the development of a child over time. In many cases, one context is the prominent contributor to an individual's sense of self-identity. For instance, a child with little family support and poor academic success may well succumb to peer pressure and join a neighborhood gang. Another child who performs well at school and has a high self-concept would be more likely to resist peer pressure. The same can be said for individuals fortunate enough to have strong family support.

Definition of Mentoring

Mentoring can be defined as a one-to-one relationship, over a pro-longed period of time, between a youth and an older person who provides consistent support, guidance and concrete help as the younger person goes through a difficult or challenging situation or period in life. The goal of mentoring is to help the mentees gain the skills and confidence to be responsible for their own futures including, and with an increasing empha-sis on, academic and occupational skills.

Transparency 1. A Conceptual Framework for Adolescent Risk Behavior: Risk and Protective Factors, Risk Behaviors, and Risk Outcomes

Interrelated Conceptual Domains of Risk Factors and Protective Factors

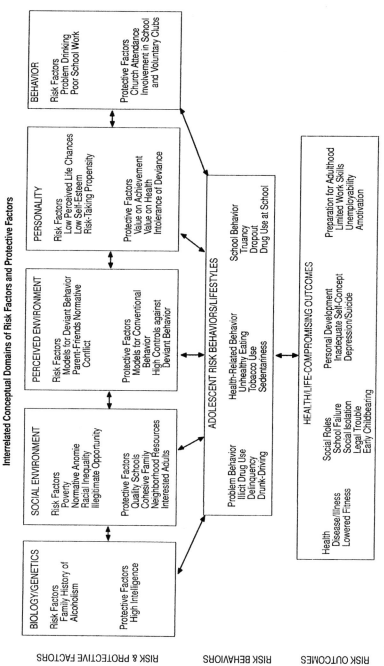

Note. From "Risk Behavior in Adolescence: A Psychosocial Framework for Understanding and Action" (p. 27) by Richard Jessor, 1992, in *Adolescents at Risk: Medical and Social Perspectives*, edited by D. E. Rogers and E. Ginzburg, Boulder, CO: Westview Press. Reprinted by permission.

73

A mentor can make a wonderful and much-needed contribution to the lives of young people in two major ways. First, a mentor can encourage a young person to dream and set future goals. Second, mentors can leave the legacy of a brighter future for a young person. *Exercise 3* and *Handout B* help to demonstrate the definition of a mentor.

The Roles of a Mentor

Mentors fulfill a wide variety of roles, but generally these roles fall into one of two categories: (1) Helping young people achieve educational or career goals; (2) Enhancing young people's awareness of and belief in their own potential. Mentors are often described as one of the following: Teachers, trainers, sponsors, talent developers, tutors, role models, advocates, coaches, counselors and friends. Use *Handout C* to help participants understand the many roles of a mentor.

The Three Stages of the Mentoring Relationship

Stage 1–Developing Rapport and Building Trust

This is perhaps the most difficult stage of the mentoring relationship. Building trust can take many, many weeks, during which time the mentees, who are often from unstable backgrounds where they were repeatedly disappointed by adults, may subject the mentors to testing. During this period, mentors can often expect unreasonable requests or sullen, moody behavior. One of the best ways to build trust is through assisting the mentee to accomplish a tangible task. Trust is an earned phenomenon. Predictability in behavior builds trust, so the mentor must attempt to be consistent. Consistency can be in the form of following through on agreements and arrangements, being on time, et cetera. In addition, it is vitally important during this stage to reassure confidentiality: Anything the mentee discloses to the mentor should be kept in confidence.

Stage 2–Reaching Goals

Once trust and rapport have been established, the mentor and mentee can get down to the serious business of striving to achieve goals. The relationship during this stage can assume any number of forms, from weekly meetings to daily telephone calls. Not all mentoring relationships are perfect, but the tangible achievement of goals maintains the energy, trust and mutual confidence in the relationship.

Stage 3–Terminating the Relationship

The majority of mentoring relationships have a termination point. This stage is just as crucial to the relationship as was the first stage. The way the relationship ends can shape how your mentee thinks about and learns from the experience. Certainly there should be a strategy and every effort to encourage mentee input on the termination.

Handout D explains in full the three stages of the mentoring relationship.

Ideal Characteristics of the Mentor

Mentors can become involved in a variety of activities which help develop a young person's full potential. Some of these include: Academic support, career development, development of self-esteem and self-confidence, dropout prevention, job search strategies, and personal growth and development. However, there are also six ideal characteristics that the mentor should focus on becoming adept in.

- *A mentor listens.* Mentors should be active listeners, encouraging young people to talk about their experiences, dreams, aspirations, concerns and feelings. Active listening helps encourage self-direction rather than direct instruction.
- *A mentor encourages.* Mentors can help the mentee build self-esteem, self-confidence and cultural pride to last a lifetime by focusing on the talents, assets and strengths of the mentee today and the realities of achieving them tomorrow. For instance, doing well in school and studying hard now will lead to the opportunity to attend college and receive a promising future.
- *A mentor builds on the positive.* The mentor should always endeavor to approach all problems and issues in a constructive, positive manner. The positive mentor can help the mentee see the connection between the dream and goal-oriented actions of today with the achievable realities of tomorrow. For instance, studying hard for school now will lead to a better chance to go to college and get a good job down the road.

- *A mentor turns everything into a learning experience.* The ideal mentor is always on the lookout for new learning opportunities and "teachable moments." If the mentee takes an interest in something, no matter how slight, every effort should be made to stimulate that interest further. Over time, the mentee may learn to be aware of and creative with his own potential.
- *A mentor advocates.* As an advocate, the mentor assumes responsibility for speaking up for the mentee in a situation where a caring adult is needed. Common areas where a mentor might advocate for his mentee include education or community and social services. As an advocate, the mentor can take full advantage of any resources available which might positively enrich the life of his or her mentee.
- *A mentor models behavior.* As a mentor, what you do is just as important as what you say. Appropriate behavior can be used to promote learning and positive development. Consistent reinforcement, persistence, and patience can all play a significant role in shaping a child's life, as well as fostering a sense of trust in adults.

Handout E should be distributed to participants to help them understand the ideal characteristics of a mentor.

Relationship Between Older Adults and Youths

Older adults and adolescents share mutual needs as well as the characteristics of having limited access to meaningful social roles, being shown a lack of respect, and craving social interaction (Cherry, Benest, Gates, & White, 1985). Both groups are experiencing periods in their lives where their previous roles must be transformed to meet new life events.

The literature indicates that a large proportion of young people grow up without the opportunity to develop relationships with caring adults (Powell & Arquitt, 1978). Intergenerational programming can serve as an intervention to meet this need as well as to allow for changes in negative perceptions and improvement in attitudes between young and old (Chapman & Neal, 1990). Older adults have the capacity to play unique and valuable roles in the lives of adolescents. They can help adolescents develop positive identities by providing the historical continuity which is essential for a fully integrated sense of self (Mead, 1974).

Upon completion of this session, *Transparency 2* can be used to reiterate the key points of the chapter.

Transparency 2

At-Risk Youths

Key Points

1. A child is **at-risk** if she or he is in danger of not achieving a productive adulthood.
2. Some issues affecting today's youths include:
    - violence/vandalism
    - substance abuse
    - poverty
    - failure in school
    - teen pregnancy
3. Warning signs that a child needs help include:
    - drug or alcohol use/abuse
    - signs of physical abuse
    - major weight loss
    - decline in academic achievement
    - law-breaking behavior
    - warning signs of suicide
4. <u>Family, school</u> and <u>neighborhood</u> all have a tremendous impact on the development of a child.

   They are each important, but one area can take up the slack if support from another is weak.

5. <u>Mentoring</u> is:
    - a one-to-one relationship
    - over a period of time
    - between a youth and an older person.
6. Mentors can help young people gain new skills as well as confidence.
7. The three stages of a mentoring relationship are:
    - developing rapport/building trust
    - reaching goals
    - terminating the relationship
8. The ideal mentor:
    - <u>listens</u>
    - <u>encourages</u>
    - is <u>positive</u>
    - turns everything into a <u>learning experience</u>
    - <u>advocates</u>
    - <u>is a model of good behavior</u>

Mentoring with At-Risk Youths

Exercises, Handouts and Transparencies

Exercise 1: Characteristics of At-Risk Youths

a. The instructor should be prepared to lead a brainstorming exercise. Using a chart to record responses, all session participants should be encouraged to contribute to the exercise. The exercise should be non-threatening with all answers recorded and none discounted. To begin the exercise the instructor should ask the question: What is an "at-risk youth?"

b. A discussion should follow with the instructor adding his/her personal insight to those expressed through the brainstorming exercise. Refer to *Handout A* to help with this exercise.

Exercise 2: Warning Signs that a Child Is At-Risk

a. This exercise should be conducted like the exercise before, with the question: What are some of the warning signs that might suggest an adolescent is in need of help?

b. Discussion as above, referring to *Handout A*.

Exercise 3: Mentoring

a. This exercise should be conducted as a brainstorming session as well. The question asked should be: What is the definition of a mentor? This question can be followed up by the question: What are some of the roles played by a mentor?

b. Discussion should follow using *Handout B* and *Handout C*.

HANDOUT A

YOUTHS IN TROUBLE

Any young person, whatever income, background, education or culture, can find themselves in trouble. Mentors cannot solve these problems, but can make a difference. Your most important roles are listening, understanding and being aware.

SIGNS THAT AN ADOLESCENT NEEDS OUTSIDE HELP

ABUSE: SEXUAL OR PHYSICAL ABUSE/INCEST/NEGLECT

ATTEMPTS AT SUICIDE

DRUG OR ALCOHOL ABUSE

Giving away possessions

Non-accidental physical injury

Making a will

Frequent "accidents"

Talking about death or dying

Abrupt changes in personality

Prolonged depression

Withdrawal

Saying her family would be better off without her

Physical defensiveness

Being suddenly at peace (may indicate a decision to end the pain by ending life)

Running away

Sudden onset of compulsive and/or self-destructive behavior

Evidence of a plan and method

Reluctance to be with a particular family member

OTHER GENERAL WARNING SIGNS

Irrational or "spaced out" behavior (sleeping a lot)

Major weight loss

A sudden increase in accidents

Poor self-image

Lying; secretiveness; alcohol on breath

Problems at school

Loss of interest in school

Serious depression

Law-breaking behavior

Severe mood swings

Spending a lot of time alone

HANDOUT B

WHAT IS MENTORING?

Mentoring is a one-to-one relationship over a prolonged period of time between a youth and an older person who provides constant support, guidance and concrete help as the young person goes through a difficult or challenging situation or period in life. The goal of mentoring is to help the mentees gain the skills and confidence to be responsible for their own futures, including, and with an increasing emphasis on, academic and occupational skills.

Mentoring is an act of community-building. It requires believing in and caring about young people–their future and ours.

Mentoring is the process of sharing personal knowledge and skills with a young person.

What Is a Mentor?

- A mentor, according to the American Heritage Dictionary, is a "wise and trusted counselor or teacher."
- The word "mentor" has a Greek root meaning steadfast and enduring.
- The ancient Greek poet Homer first coined the word "mentor" in his epic poem, *The Odyssey*. The great warrior Odysseus knew he would be away from home for many years, so he chose a man named Mentor to be the guardian and tutor of his sons. Thus, mentor came to mean any trusted counselor or guide.
- A mentor encourages the mentee to think, act and evaluate.
- A mentor praises, prods, connects and listens.
- A mentor helps a young person identify and develop their potential and shape their life.
- A mentor encourages the mentee to use their strengths, follow dreams and accept challenges.

> The true mentor fosters
> the young person's development by
> believing in him, sharing a dream
> and giving it his blessing,
> and helping to define the newly emerging
> self in its newly discovered world. (Daniel J. Levinson, 1978)

Why Mentoring?

- *Young people want support*:

  The majority of young people cite parents or other adults as the first source of advice for troubling personal problems.

- *There was a time when our society was made up of extended families and close communities*:

  Aunts, uncles, grandparents, older cousins and family friends often served naturally as mentors.

- *However, today's families are changing dramatically:*

  Nationally, nearly 15 million children live in single-parent homes.

  Almost 2.5 million children under the age of 13 are unsupervised during a part of the day.

  Only 50 percent of all custodial mothers receive full payment of court-ordered support, with 25 percent receiving nothing at all.

  One in five children lives in poverty.

  Only 40 percent of young people born in the U.S. can expect to spend their entire childhood living with both biological parents.

- *Today, adolescents are an increasingly isolated population:*

  Changes in the structure of the family, in community and neighborhood relationships and in workplace arrangements have deprived young people of the adult contacts that historically have been primary sources of socialization and support for development.

  There are fewer "natural" opportunities for youths to sustain durable relationships with adults.

  Many young people lack nurturing and supportive primary adult relationships.

  A mentor can provide that role and, perhaps more importantly, teach and guide the mentee to find others to fill that role as well.

- *For many young people, this isolation is particularly devastating:*

  Three out of 10 young people drop out of school. In many cities, more young people drop out than graduate.

  Some latch onto drug dealers and petty criminals, using these older individuals as sponsors and guides as they make their way into an alternative, illegal world of power and prestige.

- *While families bear the primary obligation to care for their children and to help them become healthy, contributing citizens and other* institutions can help families accommodate to a rapidly changing world:

A mentor can provide the nurturing, supportive adult relationship absent in the lives of many of our young people.

A Mentor Can

- Have a great impact on the life of a young person.
- Encourage a young person to dream and set goals.
- Leave the legacy of a brighter future for a young person.

What Do Mentors Gain from Mentoring?

Mentoring helps mentors to:

- Increase their regard and respect for people from different back-grounds.
- Recognize that they can make a difference.
- Feel a part of a wider community.
- Develop new friendships and relationships.
- Give back to the community through the sharing of their strengths and abilities.

Mentors and Commitment

- *A mentor must be willing to make a specified commitment of time . . . and keep to it!*
- A good mentor program must require a time commitment to enable a mentoring relationship to flourish.
- While the chemistry between two people may be the real key to a good mentoring relationship, the *quality* and *frequency* of time spent together will enhance the potential for developing a strong rapport.

What Mentors Are Not!

- A mentor is *not* a parent!
- A mentor is *not* a professional counselor!
- A mentor is *not* a social worker!
- A mentor is *not* a financier!

- A mentor is *not* a playmate!
- A mentor should *not*:
  - Break promises
  - Condone negative behavior
  - Talk down to a mentee
  - Force the mentee into anything
  - Be inconsistent
  - Become a crutch
  - Expect too much
  - Expect too little
  - Cause friction
  - Break confidentiality (except in cases of potential harm of the mentee or to other people)

HANDOUT C

WHAT ARE THE ROLES OF A MENTOR?

Mentor roles generally fall into two categories:

- Helping young people achieve educational or career goals.
- Enhancing young people's awareness of and belief in their own potential.

Mentors are commonly described as:

- Teachers
- Trainers
- Sponsors
- Developers of talent
- Tutors
- Openers of doors
- Positive role models
- Advocates
- Coaches
- Counselors
- And, of course, *friends*

Mentors are not any single one of these, but a combination depending on the characteristics and goals of the relationship.

Mentors can become involved in a variety of activities to develop a young person's full potential:

- Academic support
- Career development
- Development of self-esteem and self-confidence
- Dropout prevention
- Job-search strategies
- Personal growth and development

Most importantly:

A Mentor Listens

Mentors can encourage young people to talk about their feelings, dreams and concerns.

In the role of active listener, the mentor puts aside impulses to direct the young person in favor of encouraging a process of self-direction.

A Mentor Encourages

Mentors can help the mentee to build self-confidence, self-esteem and cultural pride to last a lifetime by focusing on the talents, assets and strengths of the mentee.

A Mentor Builds on the Positive

Whenever possible, approach the issues and problems addressed in the activities in a positive light, building on related strengths that you and your mentee may have demonstrated. For example, if reading is a problem, start by reading things in which your mentee is interested and expand from there.

You can be the one to help your mentee see the connection between her actions of today and her dreams and goals of tomorrow. For example, if your mentee dreams of graduating from high school with her classmates, be sure to point out how skipping school today will affect her chances of completing school on schedule, if at all. Bring in examples of struggles that are real to your mentee–a hero or a local community leader. Be as concrete and relevant as possible.

A Mentor Turns Everything into a Learning Experience

Keep an eye out for learning opportunities and "teachable moments." If your mentee expresses an interest in someone or something, no matter how slight, take advantage of the situation and help her develop the interest further–you never know where this might lead. Over time, she may learn to be aware of and creative with her own potential. For example, if she mentions or expresses an interest in a local politician, take her to hear the politician speak. From there, you can begin to think of other ways to transform her casual interest into other learning experiences using your time, energy and, perhaps, connections.

A Mentor Advocates

As an advocate, the mentor speaks up for the mentee in a situation where a caring adult is needed and is missing. In this role, mentors link the mentees to resources to which they have a right or might not know about or be able to take advantage of. Depending on you and your mentee's interests or goals, you may choose to advocate for your mentee in the following areas:

- *Education system*

  Is your mentee receiving the full services she is entitled to as a regular or special education student?

- *Community*

  Are there resources, programs or services available at low or no cost in which your mentee might be interested, such as summer camp?

- *Social services*

  Again, are there programs available which might help your mentee, such as tutoring, transportation or even swimming lessons?

As an advocate, you can take advantage of the connections and associations you have in the community. Are you an alumnus of a local college and/or familiar with a professor who teaches in an area in which your mentee is interested? Plan a trip to sit in on a class or meet with some of the students. Perhaps there are summer jobs or job shadowing opportunities at your office. Be creative and your mentee will learn to be creative as well.

A Mentor Models Behavior

What you do is as important as what you say, so use your behavior to promote learning and positive development in your mentee. Words reinforced by behavior are that much more powerful, especially when they are consistently reinforced by behavior. You are competing against numerous negative influences (for example, television, advertising and peers), so be persistent and patient.

If you want to promote literacy, read with your mentee at every opportunity. If you want to promote health, walk up a flight of stairs instead of taking the elevator and while you are climbing discuss with your mentee why you chose the stairs. Find creative solutions to problems your mentee brings up, encouraging discussion and the seeking out of alternatives. Engage your mentee in a discussion in which you explain the reasoning behind your behavior. The discussion, it is hoped, will prompt your mentee to discuss the reasoning behind her own behavior.

Take public transportation to an event or a museum so that your mentee will be able to get there on her own someday. Take the extra step of researching the bus line together (calling the MTA) so that she will be able to get anywhere a bus goes. This is called teaching life skills.

WHENEVER POSSIBLE

- Identify your mentee's talents, strengths and assets.
- Give recognition for effort or improvement—no matter how slight.
- Show appreciation for contribution and demonstrate confidence and faith in your mentee.
- Value your mentee no matter how she performs.
- Find and point out positive aspects of behavior.
- Suggest small steps in new or difficult tasks.
- Have reasonable expectations.
- Help your mentee use mistakes as learning experiences.

HANDOUT D

STAGES OF THE MENTORING RELATIONSHIP

The mentoring relationship typically goes through *three* stages:

Stage One: Developing Rapport and Building Trust

- *Building trust takes weeks, sometimes months.*

One of the best ways to build trust is to help your mentee quickly accomplish something tangible that is important to her. For example, assist her in following up on an interest, getting involved in a club, or meeting someone important in a career field of interest.

- *Testing may occur.*

Testing may occur, particularly when mentees are from unstable backgrounds where they have been repeatedly disappointed by adults. Testing is a form of protection from further disappointment.

Your mentee may come from a family where nothing can be taken for granted:

- People living in the household come and go.
- Frequent moves occur during the course of a year.
- The phone may be turned on and off.
- Food may be unavailable at times.

Mentees may be slow to give their trust because, perhaps based on past experience with other adults, they expect inconsistency and lack of commitment.

During the testing period, mentors can expect:

- Missed appointments
- Phone calls not returned
- Unreasonable requests
- Angry or sullen behavior

What Can Mentors Do?

Predictability builds trust, so be consistent

- Be on time for arranged meetings.
- Bring promised information and materials.
- Follow through on your agreements and arrangements with your mentee.

Provide mentees reassurance that what you discuss together is confidential

Early in the mentoring relationship, you should explain that:

- Nothing your mentee tells you will be discussed with anyone else except your program coordinator.
- If you feel that it is important to involve another adult, it will be discussed first with your mentee.
- If there is a threat of physical harm to your mentee or others, you must break confidentiality to seek protection for the endangered person(s).

Though Stage One may not be difficult in all relationships, it may be in some. It is important for you to be prepared for initial disappointments and frustration and to refrain from blaming yourself.

Stage Two: Reaching Goals

This can be a time of closeness in the relationship

- Once the testing is over, the rocky part of the relationship usually ends and exciting progress may begin to take place.

A mentoring relationship can take many forms

- The family-like relationship where you are felt to be a part of the family and contacts are frequent and intense.
- The important, less intense relationship where the focus is on accomplishing tasks. Time together is limited to weekly contact or the contact required by the mentoring program.

Any variety of these forms has its value and you may find your relationship fluctuating between them over time.

Not all mentoring relationships proceed smoothly

When things are not working, you must explore these issues:

- The fit or match may not be right.
- Your mentee may have been so disappointed and damaged by earlier experiences that she is unable to risk taking advantage of a helping relationship.
- Some mentor pairs will get stuck in the testing stage.
- You may feel burdened by the relationship and feel angry or annoyed by the youth's behaviors.

As a mentor, it is imperative that you share your experiences with and receive support from:

- The staff of your mentoring program.
- Other mentors.
- Resource persons and reference materials.

Stage Three: Terminating the Relationship

Terminating the relationship is a crucial part of the relationship

- The way the relationship ends can shape how your mentee thinks about and learns from the experience.
- Mentors should discuss strategies and guidelines for ending the relationship with the coordinators of the program.
- No matter what the strategy, if at all possible, plan ahead for the end of the relationship with your mentee. Encourage your mentee to verbalize her feelings about the termination and help her to feel supported and in control by planning future coping strategies together. Whatever you do, do not just drop out of sight.

And so it ends . . .
Much of its value may be realized—
as with love relationships generally—
after termination. The conclusion of the main
phase does not put an end to the
meaning of the relationship.
Following the separation, the younger man
may take the admired qualities of the Mentor
more fully into himself.
He may become better able to learn from himself,
or listen to the voices from within.
His personality is enriched as he makes the
Mentor a more intrinsic part of himself.
This internalization of significant figures is a
major source of development in adulthood.

Daniel J. Levinson

HANDOUT E

HOW CAN A MENTOR HELP?

- Identify the problems or symptoms.
- Seek help from the family, your program or a community resource.
- Advocate to make sure your mentee continues to receive the help she needs.

FAMILIES AND COMMUNITIES UNDER STRESS

We speak of young people being "at risk" for pregnancy, drug and alcohol abuse, failure in school and a myriad of other social problems. Many mentoring programs are initiated in response to these issues that result from people, families and communities being under stress. How can a mentor assist a young person who faces these seemingly intractable problems? What is the role of the mentor in these situations, especially when the situation is very unfamiliar to the mentor?

Be Knowledgeable

Be aware of the environment in which your mentee lives. Try to begin to understand the special stresses she may face and how these stresses may potentially affect different aspects of your mentee's life–home, school, aspirations, friendships and behavior.

- *Early childbearing*

One in eight girls under age 18 in Baltimore City will become pregnant each year. The average age of the father is 19. Teen parents are more likely to drop out of school, deliver unhealthy children and live in poverty than their peers who graduate on time.

- *Schooling*

In Baltimore City Public Schools anywhere from 40 to 80 percent of students will drop out between the ninth and twelfth grades.

- *Health*

Your mentee may have no regular source of health care or health insurance. She may have poor eating habits and no regular form of exercise or exposure to sports.

- *Home environment*

Your mentee may have no space at home for studying or keeping private things such as a journal. There may be no phone and little supervision at night or in the early morning before school. Many households are headed by a single, usually female, parent.

- *Neighborhood environment*

It may not be safe for your mentee to be out at night, so nighttime activities may be limited. Role models might consist of drug pushers and unemployed, unattached men. Homicide is the leading cause of death for black males ages 15 to 24.

- *Don't judge*

Don't limit your mentee based on her environment, but use the information to make your time with her more productive and rewarding.

- *Find the strengths*

Identify the strengths in your mentee and in her family and community. Do everything you can to help your mentee see and believe in these strengths; build on them. For example, your mentee's immediate family may be in turmoil, but there are often one or more very positive, stable role models in the extended family—perhaps an uncle or a grandparent.

Teach Life Skills

- Help your mentee learn as much as possible about the world and her own potential so that she can continue learning and growing long after you are gone.
- *Advocate* for your mentee in school, in your mentoring program, the community, and even at home when appropriate.
- *Find positive role models* next door or in the next town.
- *Support* your mentee all the way.

Chapter 8

Aging Sensitivity

Priscilla M. Kline

Learning Objective	Key Concepts/Terms	Instructor Notes
1. Discuss the importance of learning about other age groups.	Ageism; stereotyping; sensitivity training; intergenerational; generalization; discrimination	
2. Discuss the criteria on which people usually make age judgments.	Physical characteristics; limitations	Exercise 1, 2
3. Discuss common facts and myths about older people.	Individual differences	Exercise 5, Handout C, D, and F
4. Discuss the process of normal aging.	Sensory system; skin/hair pigmentation; body tissue	Handout E
5. Discuss common traits and differences between older people and other age groups.	Need for satisfying relationships	Transparency 1
6. Become familiar with, and discuss, personal feelings about older people.	Generalizations; discrimination	Exercise 3, Handout A Exercise 4; Handout B
7. Summarize key points.		Transparency 2

INTRODUCTION: AGING SENSITIVITY

The instructor should introduce him/herself and inform participants that the goal of the session is to gain knowledge and understanding about older

[Haworth co-indexing entry note]: "Aging Sensitivity." Kline, Priscilla M. Co-published simultaneously in *Activities, Adaptation & Aging* (The Haworth Press, Inc.) Vol. 23, No. 2, 1998, pp. 101-118; and: *Preparing Participants for Intergenerational Interaction: Training for Success* (ed: Melissa O. Hawkins, Francis A. McGuire, and Kenneth F. Backman) The Haworth Press, Inc., 1999, pp. 93-110. Single or multiple copies of this article are available for a fee from The Haworth Document Delivery Service [1-800-342-9678, 9:00 a.m. - 5:00 p.m. (EST). E-mail address: getinfo@haworthpressinc.com].

people. After the necessary introductions, the instructor should immediately pose several questions to enlist the youths' personal involvement in the discussion.

It is very important that the youths are actively involved in exploring, interacting and questioning, rather than just being passive recipients of knowledge. Regardless of the size of the group with whom the instructor is working, all youths should be challenged to think, respond with their own ideas, reflect on new information, and relate it to experiences they have already had or are expecting to have. Throughout the session, the instructor should engage participants' attention by asking thought-provoking questions, asking for a show of hands, and encouraging questions. It is important that the instructor acknowledge responses and facilitate universal participation. A balance between participation and over-exuberance can easily be maintained if things are kept moving, with responses being acknowledged and shared.

The sharing of personal experiences by the instructor may help the youths better understand the material that is being discussed. The youths should also be encouraged to discuss some of their experiences in dealing with older people. Discussion of personal experiences is usually lively and will help the youths relate the material to their own lives and experiences.

A discussion noting the idea of individual differences among older people, rather than mass stereotyping, may be a useful way for the instructor to end the session. To overcome stereotypes, it is necessary for the instructor to heighten awareness of older people as individuals. It is also necessary to assist youths in gaining the view of older people as people of value who have a lot to offer, as well as individuals with whom they can share and learn. The instructor should share some philosophical thoughts about what makes any person feel good to be alive, regardless of one's age. It can be pointed out that everyone laughs, everyone cries, and that all people need to have others involved in their lives. The discussion should lead specifically to the mutuality of shared experience between youths and older people.

The fact that aging is something undergone by everyone should be related to each person. Everyone will get old if he or she lives long enough! The whole notion of "older people" should take on a new and personal meaning once the trainer emphasizes this fact.

The instructor should leave participants with a thought of what is possible with new attitudes about aging and older people. The youths can look forward to learning a great deal, making new friends, and being exposed to interesting stories and unique talents gained from people who have a lifetime of experience.

"Youth is a gift of nature, but age is a work of art" (Tilka).

IMPLEMENTATION AND MATERIALS SUGGESTIONS FOR THE INSTRUCTOR

This training session is ideally suited for groups of approximately 30 participants. The instructor may arrange the room in any manner which facilitates discussion among the group; a classroom setting is preferable. If the group is small enough, the discussions may be led by only one instructor, but if the group is larger, one or two discussion leaders may be used to break the group into more manageable units. This session, depending upon the amount of participation elicited, may last two hours.

Supplies and Materials

Some things that you will or may need to conduct this training session include:

- overhead projector
- transparency markers
- extra transparencies, to make notes from the discussion for group viewing purposes
- copier (to make copies from handouts)
- flip chart or chalkboard (with markers or chalk)
- pencils for use with the handouts/questionnaires

AGING SENSITIVITY

The Importance of Learning About Other Age Groups

Often, the years that separate one generation from another contribute to ageism, the negative attitudes and misunderstandings about other age groups that frequently exist among people. In particular, the elderly have been victims of this phenomenon. Ageism was defined in 1969 as "a systematic stereotyping of and discrimination against people because they are old" (Cook, 1992). The negative views that many people hold about the elderly may not actually be a result of discriminatory attitudes, but instead a lack of knowledge about older people. In any case, these views or misconceptions should be eliminated. Older people are often viewed as mentally and physically slow, mentally or physically ill, unproductive and inactive (Jackson & Sullivan, 1987). In fact, these generalizations are often grossly incorrect. It is important to dissolve stereotypes, the oversimplified and generalized beliefs about an individual due to his or her perceived membership in a particular group, and to help youths understand and appreciate what older people are like. More frequent contact with older people can help youths have more successful and satisfying inter-generational relationships. Sensitivity training can also contribute to the reduction of the negative influence of age-related stereotyping.

What Criteria Do People Use to Judge One's Age?

Physical appearance is usually the most frequent criterion that we use to judge a person's age. The appearance of wrinkles, gray or white hair, and balding are among the most common physical characteristics that are used. In addition, a stooped posture, weak voice or visible signs of illness are often pointed to as signs of old age. However, many of these characteristics can be misleading. It is important that young people understand that although a person may exhibit some of the typical signs of aging, that person may still feel vital and young on the inside. In addition, young people should recognize that these signs of old age are not necessarily indicative of illness. Older people, in spite of gradually occurring limitations on their physical activity, may be (and often are) just as healthy as anyone else. It should be understood that judging one's ability or health simply by his or her physical appearance is stereotyping, and often these judgments are inaccurate. *Exercises 1* and *2* will help shed some light on this important topic.

Common Facts and Myths About Older People

Common stereotypes regarding aging abound in today's world. Some of these may be fact, but many are myths. In reality, older people vary as greatly as young people, and they become even more individualized as they age. The habits and idiosyncrasies that they used to keep hidden may reveal themselves in old age, as they become more comfortable with who they are.

Eighteen facts and myths about older people were adapted from Palmore's *Facts on Aging Quiz*, a list of true or false statements about older people (Palmore, 1988). For example, one myth is that most older people are senile—or that they don't have all of the mental capabilities of younger people. In fact, mental ability and accomplishments have little to do with age. As noted on *Handout D*, Ben Franklin was a newspaper columnist at the age of 16, and 65 years later helped write the United States Constitution at the age of 81. Another common myth is that many older people have to live in nursing or retirement homes. The fact is that only 5% of older people live in such institutions. Most older people are able to live their lives rather independently, without having to resort to residential care. There are many more myths that are commonly believed about older adults, and these are further discussed on *Handout D.* Additional facts and information about aging can be found on *Handout F.* Participants can complete a partial form of the *Facts on Aging Quiz* as part of *Exercise 5 (Handout C).*

The Process of Normal Aging

The process of aging is often misunderstood by younger people. Many people believe that as one grows older, one invariably gets sick, becomes forgetful, or loses most of his or her physical ability. The body does go through several changes as it grows older, but they are gradual changes and usually not exceptionally disruptive to the person's daily activities.

One normal change that the body goes through as it ages involves body tissue. As people grow older, the elastic tissue loses some of its stretch; this results in what we call wrinkles. People also notice a decline in physical strength and stamina and they will not be able to do everything that they used to do. In addition, changes occur in the sensory system. Vision, hearing, taste, touch and smell all become less sensitive as people age. This is an effect especially noticed in hearing and eyesight. Finally, changes in distribution and amount of natural skin and hair pigmentation lead to one of the most universally recognized signs of aging–gray hair.

Additional events that may mark the aging process can be found on *Handout E.*

Common Traits and Differences Between Older People and Other Age Groups

All people are individuals. This leads to differences between people, regardless of one's age. However, there are many age-related differences between people to take into account. These include physical ability and appearance distinctions as well as differences in mental ability. These differences must all be recognized if old and young people are to work together effectively, as well as have fun together. However, as pointed out on the "myth or fact?" section, these differences must not be overestimated or given too much weight. Instead, more positive attitudes toward aging should be instilled in today's youths. The fact that the elderly have a lifetime of experiences to share should be emphasized. Older people can help us learn from their mistakes, give us guidance, and even entertain us with stories of "the good old days." The differences that exist between older and younger people should be seen as a benefit rather than an obstacle. *Exercises 3* and *4*, as well as *Handouts A* and *B* can help participants examine the attitudes they hold towards older people, as well as begin to see some of the similarities that people of all ages share.

Common to all people is the feeling that we need to find meaning in our lives. Old and young people alike want to feel good about themselves and have a purpose, or a reason for living. People also share a universal need to be with others and have meaningful and gratifying relationships. By learning more about each other and sharing unique experiences and knowledge, older and younger people can form satisfying and productive affiliations. *Transparency 1* can help reiterate this philosophy to the participants, as well as lead into the summary of this session's key points *(Transparency 2)*.

Aging Sensitivity

Exercises, Handouts and Transparencies

NOTE TO INSTRUCTORS

We have provided several exercises and handouts that can be used to supplement the majority of this training session. However, all of the exercises and handouts are not necessary to have a successful program. In the case of the questionnaires, especially, it is left up to you to choose the ones that you feel most comfortable with.

Exercise 1: Age Line (Instructor Notes)

a. In this exercise, participants are asked to line up from oldest to youngest without speaking. Once in the line, ask participants to visualize their place in the continuum, in relation to the others. Then ask them to share the things that they like about being at that stage of life, as well as the things that they don't like about their age. As the group explores their feelings about being a particular age, give them the opportunity to "change" their age by moving to a new place in the line. They can also place others at the point in line where they believe the others belong.

b. Following the age-line activity (which serves to focus the group), the group should be broken down to work in small groups to identify age-related stereotypes within society. They should also examine their personal reactions to stereotypes when directed toward themselves.

The instructor is required to facilitate this activity. Discussion should be encouraged, sharing the reasons why individuals have "chosen" a new age, as well as their impressions of other ages and age stereotypes. This exercise is a particularly good "ice-breaker," if used at the beginning of the training session.

Note: This exercise is also provided for use in the Oral History chapter. It is left up to the instructor to decide where he or she would find the exercise to be most useful.

Transparency 1

Principles to Remember
People are <u>individuals.</u>

- Are all older people crotchety? NO!
- Are all older people nice? NO!
- Get to know them

Older people have a lot to offer.

- lifetime of experiences
- willing to share
- share yourself

Older people are different from you.

- respect each other
- be willing to compromise

Just like you, old people need to find meaning in their lives.

- be part of that meaning for them
- help each other find meaning together

Remember what makes you feel good to be alive.

- being liked
- recognition
- doing for others
- doing things with others

Transparency 2

Aging Sensitivity
Key Points

1. *Ageism* is the term for negative attitudes or beliefs about other age groups.

2. *Generalizations* are beliefs about an entire group based on knowledge about one or a few members of that group.

- Saying that all 60-year olds are alike is like saying that all eleven year olds are alike.

  Not true!

3. Most older people can live independently, with few limitations on their activity.

4. Most older people are not physically or mentally ill.

5. Most older people like to have work or a hobby to keep them busy.

Exercise 2: Thoughts on Older People (Instructor Notes)

This exercise is a good opening exercise, and is designed to open a discussion about older people with the participants. Simply ask the questions below and try to encourage as much discussion as possible. Stories about experiences with older people should be welcomed. The "Guess my age?" part is meant to be used like a game; a prize could be given at the end of the training session to the participant who guessed the closest to the instructor's age.

Thoughts on Older People

- How many of you have lived with an older person in your home?
- How many of you know an older person really well?
- How old is the oldest person you know?
- What makes you think someone is old?
- What do you look at to guess how old someone is?

Ask the participants to guess how old the trainer is, and reveal his or her age at the end of the session.

Exercise 3 (Instructor Notes)

This exercise involves giving a copy of *Handout A* to each participant. The questionnaire should be completed individually. Once everyone has finished, the instructor can read aloud each statement and ask participants how they answered the statements. These answers can then become the basis for discussion; the instructor can ask why a particular person answered in the way that they did, and ask how many other people answered the same way.

HANDOUT A

The following are some statements about older people. There are no right or wrong answers. Please circle the response that you feel represents your opinion.

SA = Strongly Agree
A = Agree
N = Neutral
D = Disagree
SD = Strongly Disagree

1. I like visiting old people.	SA	A	N	D	SD
2. I never want to grow old.	SA	A	N	D	SD
3. Old people get mad easily.	SA	A	N	D	SD
4. Old people are friendly.	SA	A	N	D	SD
5. It's fun to talk to old people.	SA	A	N	D	SD
6. Old people don't like to be with children.	SA	A	N	D	SD
7. Old people have a happy life.	SA	A	N	D	SD
8. Old people are mean.	SA	A	N	D	SD
9. Old people are not very smart.	SA	A	N	D	SD
10. Old people can teach me new things.	SA	A	N	D	SD
11. Old people like to boss everybody.	SA	A	N	D	SD
12. Old people don't do much.	SA	A	N	D	SD
13. Old people are stubborn.	SA	A	N	D	SD
14. Old people don't talk very much.	SA	A	N	D	SD
15. I think old people are funny.	SA	A	N	D	SD
16. Old people are sick all the time.	SA	A	N	D	SD
17. I am afraid to ride with an old driver.	SA	A	N	D	SD
18. Old people are sweet.	SA	A	N	D	SD

19. Old people are full of energy.   SA   A   N   D   SD
20. Old people laugh a lot.   SA   A   N   D   SD

Exercise 4 (Instructor Notes)

Similar in form to Exercise 3, this exercise involves having the participants complete a questionnaire, *Handout B*. When they are finished, the instructor can again lead a discussion centering on how and why the participants answered the statements in the way that they did.

HANDOUT B

For the following word pairs, circle the number on the scale that best represents your feelings towards older people. You will circle a number for each set of words.

Example: Mean   1   2   3   4   5   6   7   Nice

Circling a 6 means that you feel older people are fairly nice.

1.	Wise	1	2	3	4	5	6	7	Foolish
2.	Kind	1	2	3	4	5	6	7	Unkind
3.	Strong	1	2	3	4	5	6	7	Weak
4.	Happy	1	2	3	4	5	6	7	Sad
5.	Wrong	1	2	3	4	5	6	7	Right
6.	Selfish	1	2	3	4	5	6	7	Generous
7.	Inactive	1	2	3	4	5	6	7	Active
8.	Neat	1	2	3	4	5	6	7	Untidy
9.	Friendly	1	2	3	4	5	6	7	Unfriendly
10.	Boring	1	2	3	4	5	6	7	Interesting
11.	Productive	1	2	3	4	5	6	7	Unproductive
12.	Sick	1	2	3	4	5	6	7	Healthy
13.	Good	1	2	3	4	5	6	7	Bad
14.	Poor	1	2	3	4	5	6	7	Rich
15.	Dependent	1	2	3	4	5	6	7	Independent
16.	Calm	1	2	3	4	5	6	7	Anxious
17.	Pretty	1	2	3	4	5	6	7	Ugly
18.	Helpful	1	2	3	4	5	6	7	Harmful
19.	Clean	1	2	3	4	5	6	7	Dirty
20.	Sensitive	1	2	3	4	5	6	7	Insensitive

Exercise 5: Facts on Aging Quiz (Instructor Notes)

The *Facts on Aging Quiz* is a good way to dispel some of the common myths that many younger people hold in regards to older people. The instructor should hand out a copy of *Handout C* to each participant and allow them to complete it individually. The instructor can then use the copy of the quiz that we have completed, *Transparency 1*, as an overhead, to provide participants with the correct answers as well as some factual information. This is the only activity in this training session where the instructor may want participants to take some notes. It is up to the individual to decide whether to do this; be sure to have a comfortable writing surface available if you choose to have participants take notes. Another option would be to provide the group with copies of the completed quiz in handout form.

HANDOUT C

Facts and Myths About Older People

–adapted from Palmore's Facts on Aging Quiz

Decide whether you believe that each of the following statements is *true* or *false*, then write your answer in the blank provided.

1. The majority (more than half) of older people are senile (defective memory, disoriented, demented). _____
2. All five senses tend to decline in old age (hearing, vision, taste, smell, touch). _____
3. Lung capacity decreases in old age. _____
4. The majority of older people say that they are happy most of the time. _____
5. Physical strength tends to decline in old age. _____
6. At least 10% of older people live in longstay institutions (nursing homes, retirement homes). _____
7. Drivers over the age of 65 have more accidents per person than drivers under the age of 65. _____
8. Older workers cannot work as effectively as younger workers. _____
9. About 80% of older workers say they are healthy enough to carry out their normal activities. _____
10. The reaction time of older people tends to be slower than that of younger people. _____

11. Older people tend to take longer to learn something new. _____
12. The majority of older people are unable to adapt to change. _____
13. In general, older people tend to be pretty much alike. _____
14. The majority of older people say they are usually bored. _____
15. The majority of older people say they are lonely. _____
16. Over 15% of the United States population is now aged 65 or older. _____
17. The majority of older people have incomes below the poverty level. _____
18. The majority of older people say they would like to have some kind of work to do. _____

HANDOUT D

Facts and Myths About Older People

—adapted from Palmore's Facts on Aging Quiz

1. The majority (more than half) of older people are senile.　　　**F**

(defective memory, disoriented, demented)

- The majority are normal in thinking, with perhaps some forgetfulness or memory loss.
- Depending on age and illness, some experience dementia or senility, but even at extreme old age, the number is fewer than 30%.
- Mental ability and accomplishments have little to do with age.
- Ben Franklin was a newspaper columnist at 16 and helped write the constitution at 81.
- Prime ministers of the world have included England's William Pitt (age 24) and Israel's Golda Meir (age 71).
- George Bernard Shaw was 94 when one of his plays was first produced.

2. All five senses tend to decline in old age.　　　**T**

(hearing, vision, taste, smell, touch)

The extent and types of changes vary from one person to another, but all can occur normally with aging. Some people show more decline than others.

Vision

Beginning in the 40s, small objects are harder to focus on clearly. Fine print and small instrument gauges are harder to see.

- Glasses or a magnifying lens may be necessary.
- Reaction time (accommodation) decreases; it takes longer to shift focus from near to far.
- Side vision may decrease; may become necessary to turn head from side to side.
- Glare from bright light may be temporarily blinding.
- Ability to discriminate between light and dark decreases.

Hearing

- Decreased perception of higher frequencies can occur.
- To help an older person hear you, you don't necessarily have to talk louder; lower your pitch and slow your speed. Also look directly at the person and do not mumble.

Taste

- Up to 2/3 of the taste buds may be lost with aging.
- The longest lasting taste is usually sweet, and maybe metallic. Salty, bitter and sour tastes, however, decrease.
- Older people may need spices added to foods to enhance their flavor.

Smell

- Smell is decreased in half of the people aged 65 to 85.
- The decrease in smell affects both the taste and enjoyment of foods.
- However, this may mean that an older person is less sensitive to things such as body odor!

3. Lung capacity decreases in old age.   T

- Lung muscle fibers decrease in number, bulk, size and efficiency. Breathing depends on the muscles, and therefore can be harder to accomplish. Older people may become short of breath.
- Regular exercise throughout life can slow this process, however; many older people are in better shape than younger ones.

4. The majority of older people say they are happy most   **T**
of the time.

- If an older person is unhappy, she or he may have always been un-happy. Age doesn't change that.
- Older people may become depressed for many reasons, such as losses, physical illnesses, or regrets over the past.

5. Physical strength tends to decline in old age.   **T**

- Muscle fibers decrease in size, number and efficiency.
- Strength and endurance may be decreased; fatigue can occur more easily.
- Older people can cope with focusing on the important tasks, pacing themselves, and taking more frequent rest periods.

6. At least 10% of older people live in longstay institutions   **F**
(nursing homes, retirement homes).

- Only 5% of older people live in residential elderly institutions.
- More older people live in their own homes (71%) than do younger people (63%).

7. Drivers over the age of 65 have more accidents per person   **F**
than drivers under age 65.

While many older drivers are slower, the accident rates for older people are actually better.

8. Older workers cannot work as effectively as younger workers.   **F**

- Knowledge is stored over a lifetime. The attitudes and use of one's knowledge are what make the difference for any worker.
- Based on experience and judgment, better planning can make up for speed. Knowing how to approach work can lead to accuracy without having to make mistakes first.

9. About 80% of older workers say they are healthy enough   **T**
to carry out their normal activities.

The majority of older people are still in relatively good health.

10. The reaction time of older people tends to be slower than   **T**
that of younger people.

- Slower nerve conduction in older people leads to slower reflexes.
- Older people are slower to think and make decisions, even though their memory may be excellent.
- Thinking is based on the life pattern; "use it or lose it." If one is highly intelligent, usually less deterioration is lost or noticed.

11. Older people tend to take longer to learn something new.   **T**

- The taking in and processing of new information may be difficult, and older people may need more decision time. However, new learning is possible, even if it is slower.
- Memory for the past is relatively untouched; older people have good stories to tell!

12. The majority of older people are unable to adapt to change. **F**

- Older people simply need time to process information, since reaction time may be slower.
- They also need to understand the relevance and reasons for change.

13. In general, older people tend to be pretty much alike.   **F**

- No two people are the same, and people grow even more different as they develop.
- To say all older people are alike is like saying that all people of any group are alike.
- Experiences, personalities, and life in general shape each of us so that we become more unique, individualized . . . *ourselves.*

14. The majority of older people say they are usually bored.   **F**

Most older people are actually busy, active, and have many interests. To find out what they enjoy doing, all you have to do is ask.

15. The majority of older people say they are lonely.   **F**

This is also not true.

16. Over 15% of the United States population is now aged   **F**
65 or older.

Currently 12.5% of U.S. citizens are over the age of 65; this number is growing.

17. The majority of older people have incomes below the   **F**
poverty level.

There are 31 million people in the U.S. over the age of 65. However, only 4 million are below the poverty level, and 2 million are near the poverty level.

18. The majority of older people say they would like to have   **T**
some kind of work to do.

- In 1950, nearly half of all people over the age of 65 still worked. In 1970, less than one-fourth did.
- Many people retire, but more are taking second jobs or doing some type of volunteering. They do this because they want to have something worthwhile to do.

Handout E: The Normal Aging Process (Instructor Notes)

Handout E can be used as supplemental information to be given to the participants. It can also be used as a basis for discussion. Ask the group if they can list some of the things that happen to the body as a person ages, and try to encourage specific examples that they might have seen in relatives, neighbors, etc. If the *Facts on Aging Quiz* has just been administered and discussed, the group should already have some of the events that mark the aging process fresh in their minds.

HANDOUT E

The Normal Aging Process

After the age of 21 or so, brain cells begin to die. Eventually for some people, memory may be lost.

There are trillions of brain cells in the normal brain, but most of us never use them all and don't notice when we start losing them.

The protein synthesis alters and cells stop being restored, so they die.

Elastic tissue: connects body tissues throughout the body; its effects vary as it loses some function and some of its stretch. This leads to wrinkles.

Muscle fibers: these become fewer in number, less in size and less efficient. This happens to all muscles in the body. Can contribute to fatigue. The heart, which is a muscle, has a rate decrease, which can result in changes in blood pressure.

Nerve conduction: becomes less effective.

Nerve conduction sees a decrease in velocity by about 15% and also a decrease in nerve reaction time.

Sensory System

See *Handout D.*

Body Mass

Fat tissue under skin decreases, as does bone density. The decrease in bone density can result in a greater potential of injury.

A curving of the spine can lead to decreased height and stooping.

Sweat gland production declines, leading to less sweat, even when hot.

Decreased pigmentation in the skin and hair leads to gray hair.

*Other changes in the body may occur, but these are due to illness and not aging.

Psychological and Social Changes

Older people, as they maintain and develop their lifelong personality traits, become more *themselves.*

Handout F: More Facts on Aging (Instructor Notes)

Similar to *Handout E*, this handout is provided mainly as supplemental information. It does, however, contain some interesting facts that the instructor may want to highlight as a part of the session discussion.

HANDOUT F

More Facts on Aging

Older people are the fastest growing part of our population. This is due to:

1. better health care
2. better technology
3. longer life expectancy

In 1980, there were three young people to every one older person. Soon the numbers will be equal.

The life expectancy has and will continue to change:

Year 1000	25 years
1776	35
1900	40-50
1985	75

*right now, the average life expectancy is 73 for males, 80 for females

by 2000	90-95

Women outlive men!

However, there are 125 males born for every 100 females.

Old age is something that happens to all of us, if we live long enough.

We do wear out and wear down, but no one knows exactly why (yet).

Chapter 9
Racial and Ethnic Understanding

Alvin Larke, Jr.
Melissa O. Hawkins

Learning Objective	Key Concepts/Terms	Instructor Notes
1. Discuss the meaning of prejudice and its impacts.	prejudice; sensitivity; misperceptions; hatred; bias	Transparency 1 Exercise 1, Handout A
2. Explain the meaning of ethnic diversity.	stereotype; ethnocentrism; racism; diversity	Transparency 2, Exercise 2
3. Discuss the importance of multicultural education.	multicultural	Transparency 3, 4, 5, and 6
4. Introduce a model of cultural sensitization.	"self" vs. "others"	Transparency 7
5. Discuss the importance of communication.	Tolerance	Transparency 8 and 9; Exercise 3, Handout B
6. Summarize key points.		Transparency 10

RACIAL AND ETHNIC UNDERSTANDING

The instructor should introduce him or herself, welcome the participants, and explain that this session aims to educate them and make them aware of the following: all people have prejudices; all people are different from each other; and without prejudices, people are able to get along and

---

[Haworth co-indexing entry note]: "Racial and Ethnic Understanding." Larke, Alvin, Jr. and Melissa O. Hawkins. Co-published simultaneously in *Activities, Adaptation & Aging* (The Haworth Press, Inc.) Vol. 23, No. 2, 1998, pp. 119-129; and: *Preparing Participants for Intergenerational Interaction: Training for Success* (ed: Melissa O. Hawkins, Francis A. McGuire, and Kenneth F. Backman) The Haworth Press, Inc., 1999, pp. 111-121. Single or multiple copies of this article are available for a fee from The Haworth Document Delivery Service [1-800-342-9678, 9:00 a.m. - 5:00 p.m. (EST). E-mail address: getinfo@haworthpressinc.com].

111

work with one another better. Providing participants with the necessary skills to utilize their new knowledge is also an intent of this session. It should be explained to the participants that they will not be required to reveal any of their prejudices or biases during this session.

In any setting combining people who do not know one another, an awkwardness exists that can only be overcome by the passing of time, as individuals come to know and learn about one other. People are shaped by their cultural backgrounds, life experiences, and physical attributes. Diversity in these characteristics often alienates people from each other simply because of misperceptions. Admittedly, some individuals choose to remain separate from others for reasons of prejudice or hatred.

A training unit in racial and ethnic understanding is imperative because of the potential diversities between the older and younger groups, as well as within the generations. Most people hold a number of preconceived notions and various misperceptions. Training in ethnic sensitivity can facilitate positive interactions, group cohesion, and greater understanding among all project participants.

Training in ethnic and racial sensitivity is important, especially if there is a great deal of diversity among the participants of any given project. Slight modifications in the terminology or hypothetical examples may be made in order to tailor the session to the participants' knowledge or experience levels. Whether or not to make any modifications will be left up to the instructor.

IMPLEMENTATION AND MATERIALS SUGGESTIONS FOR THE INSTRUCTOR

This training session is ideally suited for approximately 30 to 50 participants. The instructor may arrange the room in any manner which facilitates discussion among the group. This session, depending on the amount of participation elicited, may last approximately three to four hours.

Supplies and Materials

Some things that you will or may need to conduct this training session include:

- overhead projector
- transparency markers
- extra transparencies
- copier (to make copies from handouts)
- flip chart or chalkboard (with markers or chalk)
- pencils for use with handouts

RACIAL AND ETHNIC UNDERSTANDING

The Meaning of Prejudice and Its Impacts

Prejudice is a preconceived judgment or opinion formed without just grounds or before sufficient knowledge. All people have prejudices and biases. All people are different from each other. Without prejudices, people are able to get along and work with one another more cooperatively.

Understanding the concept of sensitivity is key in developing skills which will dissolve prejudicial barriers. Sensitivity is the delicate awareness of the attitudes and feelings of others. People vary as to appearance, age, social class, disability, race, and gender. When people are sensitive to these differences, they are able to realize that such attributes bear no importance in personal relationships or interactions.

Often, the reasons certain people or groups are treated differently is because they possess characteristics that are foreign to others. For example, sometimes treatment is based on the way a person looks, his/her cultural background, or his/her material possessions. However, the impacts of prejudice go beyond differential treatment. Prejudice can be passed down through generations of families, resulting in a mind set which is nearly unchangeable. *Transparency 1*, *Exercise 1* and *Handout A* should be used in conjunction with this material.

What Is Ethnic Diversity?

Ethnic diversity refers to the various groups in society who possess differing customs, languages, and/or social values. Individuals form groups based on characteristics that are similar across each individual involved. Groups may form based on ethnic origin, race, age, or professional affiliation. Groups differ in attitudes and behaviors and are established around such structures as churches and schools. They have different names and vary in preference with regard to boundaries of space.

A group's name is a valued source of its identity. Group names are similar in meaning to personal names, in that they evoke a sense of pride, just as individuals take pride in their personal identifiers given to them at birth. Purposefully using slanderous names, misspelling, or mispronouncing names is prejudicial behavior.

Individuals who are members of groups carry the groups' characteristics outside of the group setting. This may lead to stereotyping. Stereotyping occurs when a group is characterized in a negative light because the behavior of one of its members is assumed to be the norm for the rest of the group.

Transparency 1

**Becoming
Sensitized**

HANDOUT A

1. List your favorite things about yourself.
2. What are your three favorite foods?
3. List the activities that you like to do on the weekends.
4. What is your favorite color?
5. What is your favorite animal?
6. Where do you like to vacation?

Groups differ in preference with regard to boundaries of space. In many cultures, there is an unspoken rule regarding the comfortable amount of space that people leave between themselves when they are conversing. However, groups vary on these boundaries. Some groups are extremely affectionate, while others are distant and rarely touch one another. When individuals from an affectionate group and an unaffectionate group come in contact, they are often uncomfortable interacting with one another.

Racism is defined as a system of privilege and penalty based on one's race. It consists of two facets: a belief in the inherent superiority of some people and inherent inferiority of others, and the acceptance of the way goods and services are distributed in accordance with these judgments. Ethnocentrism is defined as a set of discriminatory beliefs and behaviors based on ethnic differences. Use *Transparency 2* and *Exercise 2* to emphasize the importance of ethnic diversity.

Multicultural Education

Multicultural education is a philosophy and a process in which acceptance and respect for human diversity is emphasized (Mills, 1983). Although Mills (1983), specifically addresses the formal education system, education in multicultural issues can and should take place in any setting and with individuals of any age who are going to be involved with others who are ethnically different from themselves. Multicultural education teaches people the importance of being cognizant of more than just skin colors, backgrounds, and religious beliefs. The goal of educating people is to eliminate the preconceived notions and prejudices that all individuals hold.

When working with youths in ethnic sensitivity training, involving the parents is beneficial. Parents need to be informed of what their children are being taught. Developing an understanding of multicultural education can aid the parents in their own relationships with others, and can also help them understand their children better.

Transparency 2

Ethnic Diversity

- All of us have prejudices and biases.
- Groups differ in attitudes and behaviors.
- Groups have different names.
- Groups differ on boundaries of space.

It should be understood that the "ideal" family does not exist. Some parents may be leery of multicultural education. Like everyone, parents are from varying life situations and class systems.

If ethnic and racial understanding is to be infused among society members, materials which depict diversity must be available, attainable, and emphasized. The time devoted to recognizing minority populations should not be limited; i.e., Black History Month. Historical references to different ethnic groups should be encouraged, not forgotten. Society must communicate across racial, gender, class, and age barriers if its members are to live in a diverse and productive nation. *Transparencies 3, 4, 5* and *6* should be this material.

Transparency 3

**Multicultural
Education**

**"A philosophy and a process by which
schools demonstrate acceptance and
respect for human diversity. . ."**

Transparency 4

**Multicultural
Education**

**". . . an education system must be
cognizant of more than the skin colors,
backgrounds, and religious beliefs of
people."**

Transparency 5

**Multicultural
Education**

**"[Educational systems] must educate to
eliminate classism, racism, sexism, ageism, handicappism . . . and uglyism."**

Transparency 6

**Infusing
Multiculturalism
Tips**

- Select textbooks and materials that depict diversity.
- Don't limit the recognition of minorities to one month out of the year.
- Don't leave groups in the past.
- Use the "Teachable Moment!"
- Mandate Multicultural Education courses.

Introduce a Model of Cultural Sensitization

In Larke's (1990) model of cultural sensitization, the "self" and "others" are represented by large circles. They overlap at the model's center to represent a culturally sensitive person. This model illustrates how all individuals possess varying generalizations, attitudes, and preconceptions about others. These attitudes can be about dress, gender roles, hygiene, traditions, or any number of things. *Transparency 7* depicts Larke's Model of Cultural Sensitization.

The Importance of Communication

Communication is vital to one's positive and productive involvement with others. It can be a difficult process which often requires patience and tolerance. Communication can be hindered when the people with whom one is communicating are different from him/her in some capacity. Examples of the issues involved in communicating with students and parents are given because of the commonalty of these groups in society.

It must be remembered that appearances can be deceiving. Often the manner in which one communicates, whether it be through action, dress, speech, or body language, causes others to be confused. This is often the case with the youths population.

Judgments about others are often made based on appearance. People may find that they are treated better in restaurants and stores when they dress a certain way. Sometimes messages are misinterpreted. When they

Transparency 7

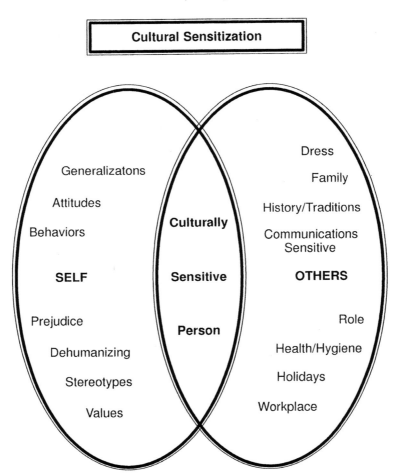

Cultural Sensitization

Generalizatons

Attitudes

Behaviors

SELF

Prejudice

Dehumanizing

Stereotypes

Values

Culturally

Sensitive

Person

Dress

Family

History/Traditions

Communications
Sensitive

OTHERS

Role

Health/Hygiene

Holidays

Workplace

are not sent at all, people still form impressions. Examples leading to misinterpretations may include degree of eye contact, comfort zone level, and flamboyant dress. *Transparencies 8* and *9, Exercise 3* and *Handout B* should be used to further explain this material.

Upon completion of this chapter, *Transparency 10* can be used to summarize the key points of the session.

Transparency 8

Communicating with Students

- Not all minority students are athletes.
- Understand differences in eye contact.
- Some groups value sharing and cooperation.
- All students need a comfort zone.

Transparency 9

Communicating with Parents: Concerns

- Classism.
- Parents may be paranoid or intimidated.
- Single parents.

Racial and Ethnic Understanding

Exercises, Handouts and Transparencies

Exercise 1: Everyone Is Different (Instructor Notes)

Each person should complete *Handout A* individually. Then, each individual may share their answers during the discussion.

The instructor should emphasize the fact that preferences vary greatly. One person may prefer fish to spaghetti, while the opposite may be true for another person. It will become obvious that everyone in the group is different in one way or another. Similarly, it will become evident that these differences do not matter.

Transparency 10

**Racial and Ethnic
Understanding**

Key Points

1. Prejudice is a preconceived judgement or opinion formed about some-one without just grounds or before sufficient knowledge.

2. Sensitivity is the delicate awareness of the attitudes and feelings of others.

3. A group's name is a valuable source of its identity.

4. Cultural groups differ in many respects. One of these is in their differing needs for personal space.

5. Racism consists of two parts:

   - a belief in the superiority of some people and the inferiority of others; and
   - the acceptance of the distribution of goods and services in accordance with these beliefs.

6. Appearances can be deceiving!

Exercise 2: Groups in Society (Instructor Notes)

For this exercise, have participants stand up, choose a partner, and begin talking about what they are planning to do the next day. Let them talk for several minutes and then ask them to freeze in the positions they are in. Ask them to observe one another and themselves. They should observe how close they are standing to one another, as well as their body position, and hand placement. Tell the participants to observe the other groups to notice how close they got to each other in conversation. Any differences should be recognized by the participants so that they will understand how, as individuals in different ethnic groups, they differ from one another. The questions outlined in this exercise will serve as a discussion guide for the instructor. Ask the group if they encountered any discomfort in their conversations because their partner preferred a different range of closeness than she or he did. Point out that because of their different cultures, certain groups of individuals may feel more comfortable with very little space between themselves and the person(s) with whom they are talking. The reverse may be true for people of other cultures.

HANDOUT B

1. Do you get treated better in restaurants when you dress a certain way? When are you treated the best?

2. Have you witnessed judgments being made based on someone's appearance? Please describe them.

3. Have you ever made a mistake about someone because you misinterpreted their dress, degree of eye contact, or the manner in which they spoke? List examples of this based on your personal experiences or observations.

Groups in Society

Do you feel you're standing too close to the person with whom you are talking?

Are there differences in proximity among other pairs in the room?

Do you feel that you would be uncomfortable talking in this manner to other people in the room?

Exercise 3: Are Judgments Based on Appearances? (Instructor Notes)

Each person should complete *Handout B* individually, and then share their answers in a group discussion.

Chapter 10

Introduction to Groups

Susan Wilson
Bonnie Stevens

Coming together in a group with the goal of accomplishing a task is not an easy endeavor. Individuals bring to the group their own thoughts, feelings and ideas which may help or hinder the progress of the group. Resigning individuality to a group while retaining the uniqueness that enables one to contribute is not simple. Yet teams of individuals are important because they maximize effort (Garrison & Bly, 1997). In order to accomplish the job at hand, a group leader must be aware of and understand the dynamics involved in both the individuals that make up a group and the group itself. How a group of people interacts has a large impact on the success or failure of a group or the task the group is seeking to accomplish. The proper development of a group at its onset can prevent conflict, increase productivity, and ease the burden on the group leader and the individual group members. The concept of synergy indicates that the group cohesion, group morale and level of group productivity will impact one another and as these components are enhanced, they will positively affect each other. Conversely, when they are lower, they will negatively impact each other (Fuoss & Troppmann, 1981). Therefore impacting one "ingredient" to group success will add to the "recipe" for success. Understanding and developing group dynamics enables a team to communicate, problem-solve and resolve conflict to ensure the success of the task. A leader who facilities group cohesiveness through team building exercises

[Haworth co-indexing entry note]: "Introduction to Groups." Wilson, Susan, and Bonnie Stevens. Co-published simultaneously in *Activities, Adaptation & Aging* (The Haworth Press, Inc.) Vol. 23, No. 3, 1999, pp. 131-134; and: *Preparing Participants for Intergenerational Interaction: Training for Success* (ed: Melissa O. Hawkins, Francis A. McGuire, and Kenneth F. Backman) The Haworth Press, Inc., 1999, pp. 123-126. Single or multiple copies of this article are available for a fee from The Haworth Document Delivery Service [1-800-342-9678, 9:00 a.m. - 5:00 p.m. (EST). E-mail address: getinfo@ haworthpressinc.com].

123

and communication skill development will find that the synergy level will be raised and team conflict will be reduced (Russell, 1986).

INDIVIDUALS

An individual is a collection of such things as personality, demographics (i.e., gender, age), culture, upbringing, and values (Alder & Towne, 1996). People bring different strengths, weaknesses and motivations to the groups they join. Maintaining some degree of individuality and distinctiveness among members helps assure that groups will not develop a collective mentality with negative consequences such as group think. Group think occurs when members achieve a consensus without fully considering all potential outcomes of their decisions (Garrison & Bly, 1997). Groups, however, are not just collections of individuals. A successful group is one that is homogenous in its purpose while retaining individual heterogeneity (Garrison & Bly, 1997). Members of a team need to feel a sense of safety, belongingness, and identity within a group but they also need to be personally appreciated and challenged (Alter & Towne, 1996 and Lussier, 1996).

GROUPS

A group can be defined as two or more individuals interacting to achieve a goal (Lussier, 1993). Individuals join together in groups for a variety of reasons, including task completion and socialization. Membership in the group may be short or long-term and motivated by an array of reasons. Regardless of their composition or purpose, groups have characteristics including cohesiveness, morale, norms, structure, and productivity (Kraus, Carpenter, & Bates, 1981). Understanding these characteristics and how they contribute to a particular group's culture is valuable to the leader and the team as a whole. Group cohesiveness is the draw that brings individuals together and keeps them interested in each other and the team. Group morale is the perception that the team has of itself and is dependent on the satisfaction the group experiences. Norms are the shared expectations of members' behavior (Lussier, 1993) and define which behaviors are acceptable and which are inappropriate. The structure of a team is its formal and informal makeup. Structure determines leadership and the roles each member of the group will play. Each group has goals, and the extent to which these goals are met is the degree of productivity within a team.

The characteristics of a group will impact success. Understanding the vital segments of a team will aid in the development and maintenance of the group (Lussier, 1993).

COMMUNICATION

Communication is crucial to the development and survival of any group (Johnson & Johnson, 1982; Russell, 1986; Lussier, 1986; Jordan, 1997 and; Paulus, Seta, & Baron, 1996). Effective teams are able to communicate their goals to their members and to society. Free and honest communication among members allows for an open exchange of thoughts and emotions (Johnson & Johnson, 1984). Creating a non-threatening environment for communication requires the development of a setting in which members feel comfortable enough to be straight-forward without being excessively critical in their feedback of other members. Communication among members impacts every characteristic of a group (Lussier, 1996). Two-way communication requires group members listen and offer appropriate responses. This can only be accomplished when participants accept and appreciate each other (Lussier, 1996).

Problem solving and decision making, key aspects of a group's success, require a high degree of communication (Johnson & Johnson, 1984). Feedback enables a group to examine outcomes and alter performance to achieve desired goals (Haslett & Ogilivie, 1996). Modification to a group's structure or approach is usually done to accommodate some transformation to the group, its purpose, or the society it serves. This change requires that the entire group understand and agree with these adjustments to minimize the effect on the groups' cohesiveness, morale, norms, structure, or productivity.

Alterations to a group's structure or purpose leave it open to conflict. Communication is significant in the development of a group, yet its most vital role may be in the maintenance of the team. One barrier to continuance of a group is conflict within the group. Communication can facilitate a reduction in conflict and can assist in resolution of issues (Lussier, 1996). Knowledge of group and interpersonal dynamics enables the group members to reconcile issues and address the substantial concerns endangering the group.

CONCLUSION

Knowledge of the factors influencing the formation, development and operation of groups is crucial to creating effective teams. Successful group leaders will understand the role of individuals and communication in operation of groups. This chapter will introduce essential concepts of group dynamics and provide the reader with activities that may be used to build strong groups.

Chapter 11

Group Dynamics

Jack L. Stevenson
Paul S. Wright

Learning Objective Notes	Key Concepts/Terms	Instructor
1. Introduce basic concept of group dynamics.	Group processes	
Discuss the significance of groups.	Primary and secondary groups; status and roles	
Describe the importance of understanding the EIAG Model.	Experience; identify; analyze; generalize	Exercise 1 Handout A
2. Discuss how listening is a dynamic activity.	Listening: activity steps	Exercise 2 Handout B Handout C
3. Discuss the importance of feelings as basic motivations of human behavior.	Feelings: happy, afraid; hurt; angry; interested; fearless; eager; doubtful	Exercise 3
4. Discuss levels of group functioning.	Stroking; organizing; producing; creating	Exercise 4
Discuss the importance of understanding group properties	Universal characteristics: purpose; tone or social atmosphere; cohesion; organizational structure; patterns of communication; patterns	

[Haworth co-indexing entry note]: "Group Dynamics" Stevenson, Jack L., and Paul S. Wright. Co-published simultaneously in *Activities, Adaptation & Aging* (The Haworth Press, Inc.) Vol. 23, No. 3, 1999, pp. 135-169; and: *Preparing Participants for Intergenerational Interaction: Training for Success* (ed: Melissa O. Hawkins, Francis A. McGuire, and Kenneth F. Backman) The Haworth Press, Inc., 1999, pp. 127-161. Single or multiple copies of this article are available for a fee from The Haworth Document Delivery Service [1-800-342-9678, 9:00 a.m. - 5:00 p.m. (EST). E-mail address: getinfo@ haworthpressinc.com].

	of interaction; procedures; internal commitment; group history	
5. Introduce essential group roles according to their function.	Group building and maintenance roles; group task roles	
Discuss the concept of negative roles.	Aggressive behavior; blocking; special interest pleading; withdrawing; clowning	
Introduce the diversity in group membership roles.	Group membership roles	
6. Discuss the difference between internal and external force.	Cluster A; Cluster B; Cluster C forces	
7. Introduce observational guidelines which help analyze group behavior.	Participation; style of influence; decision-making procedures; task functions; maintenance functions; group atmosphere; membership; feelings; norms	Handout D Handout E
Discuss the elements of effective group-decision making.	Group harmony; happy members; group process; effective groups; personal inventory; individual and group skills	
8. Discuss positive conflict resolution.	Positive power moves; rational approaches; creative interchange.	Exercise 5 Handout F
Introduce the concept of creative interchange.	Interacting; appreciating; integrating; expanding through facilitation increased knowledge; increased value; increased control; increased community	Handout G
9. Summarize key points.		Transparency 1 (Following Transparency do Exercise 6)

INTRODUCTION: GROUP DYNAMICS

The instructor should begin with an introduction of him/herself and discuss why the group should be interested in learning something about group dynamics. If participants are planning to embark on a project which requires extensive group interaction then the instructor should be sensitive to this and structure the session accordingly. For example, if participants' interaction is to include committee work or specific task-oriented endeavors then the instructor should attempt over the course of the session to provide tangible examples of situations and scenarios that might later confront the participants. It should be emphasized that a basic understanding of group processes is fundamental to the success of any group in any given situation. By introducing potential groups to positive and negative group roles and levels of group functioning, participants can learn how to be effective contributors to the group and provide for optimal group functioning.

The subject of group dynamics is covered in great detail over the course of the next few pages. The individual chosen to conduct a training session in this area should have some background in this area. What follows is a comprehensive resource to aid the instructor in developing or structuring a training session in group dynamics. In the interests of time and possible information overload, the instructor should be prepared to select only what he/she feels is most important for participants to know. As far as is possible each session should attempt to generate participant enthusiasm and provide for a great deal of group interaction. The session should be planned carefully facilitating contributions from all group members. Handouts should be provided to give participants a point of reference and a resource to carry away at the conclusion of the session.

IMPLEMENTATION AND MATERIALS SUGGESTIONS FOR THE INSTRUCTOR

This training session is ideally suited for small groups (15-30 people), however it can be structured to accommodate much larger groups. Space and numbers permitting, seating arrangements should be made so that everyone is seated in a circle with space at one point for the instructor and a flip chart. For larger groups, seating arrangements should be made such that everyone is seated facing the front of the room. It is important that there be ample space whereby groups can easily break up into smaller groups when required. Tables and desks are obstacles to effective group discussion and where possible should be removed from the room. This training session can last from between three and five hours, depending on the depth of discussions and the specificity of the presented material.

Supplies and Materials

A suggested list of supplies and materials needed to conduct this training session include:

- overhead projector
- transparency markers
- extra transparencies, to make notes from the discussion for viewing purposes

- copier (to make copies of handouts)
- flip chart or chalk board (with markers or chalk)
- boxes of pens and pencils for participants
- notepads for participants

GROUP DYNAMICS

Basic Concepts Guiding Group Dynamics

Group Dynamics is the study of how individuals effectively, or ineffectively, function as a group. A large number of different disciplines contribute to effective group functioning. For instance, group dynamics demands a basic understanding of leadership styles, communication skills, decision-making processes, interpersonal facilitation, organizational behavior, and conflict resolution.

The purpose of training in group dynamics is to break down barriers between people and to facilitate a sense of cohesiveness among members of a group. In all human interactions there are two major ingredients–content and process. The first, content, deals with the subject matter or the task upon which the group is working. The second ingredient, process, is concerned with what is happening between and to group members while the group is working. *Group dynamics* deals with such items as morale, feeling, tone, atmosphere, influence, participation, styles of influence, leadership struggles, conflict, cooperation, et cetera. In most interactions, very little attention is given to process, even when it is the major cause of ineffective group action. Sensitivity to group processes will better enable one to diagnose group problems early and deal with them more effectively.

To understand group processes, one must be aware of the following characteristics of groups:

1. A group has more information than an individual.
2. Group characteristics such as size, atmosphere, flexibility, homogeneity, cohesiveness, and leadership exist in equilibrium. Changing one aspect changes *all* aspects.
3. Groups may change and undergo processes through time.
4. A group has more than one point of view.
5. A group is synergetic. Members are influenced and stimulated by each other.
6. Group member participation and satisfaction increase as group trust increases.

7. Individuals try to influence the group. Power is an essential aspect of each and every group.

In addition to the above group dynamics, the student should also be made aware of the seven characteristics of an *effective group*:

1. Discussions involve all members in the content of the group discussions.
2. An environment of openness and trust exists.
3. There is free expression of ideas and feelings.
4. A cooperative, friendly, supportive environment exists.
5. Members enjoy their participation.
6. Members are interested.
7. The group is small enough to permit participation by all members.

The Significance of Groups

Groups tell us who we are, what we can do, and how we are to behave. We are members of many groups simultaneously. In each we have a function, derive some strength or support, and perform some acts. Some groups are more critical to our emotional and physiological development than others; some are short-lived; some are a part of us throughout our lives. In their attempt to describe the role played by groups, sociologists have divided them into two major categories, *primary* and *secondary.*

Primary groups are essential to the development of our personality, our value system, and our patterns or response. The family is the basic primary group. From it and its members we learn to react in specific, predictable patterns to various situations and stimuli. Our response to family members is both intellectual and emotional. Subconsciously, we model much of our behavior after our parents, the way they perform their roles and responsibilities. Primary groups are long-lasting in their effect and are characterized by an emotional interdependency, one for another.

Secondary groups are more numerous than the primary ones. Membership in them may be temporary or long-term; responses to other members of the group tend to be more intellectual than emotional. Secondary groups provide us with opportunities for achievement and recognition and become avenues for meeting many of our basic social needs. They usually form around some task or social function, such as work or worship. Whereas the primary group experiences shape our personality and emotional character, secondary groups polish our behavior and socialize us. Most organized recreation experiences occur in a secondary group setting.

Groups both condition and stimulate our behaviors. In them, we learn what to do and what is expected of us; in other words, we assume certain roles and perceptions. In each group we have *status*, and our perception of that status dictates our performance. Of course, the way we act is conditioned by previous group experiences that we tend to use as references. We continually monitor and modify our behavior depending on the way those we respect respond to our performance; they become our "critical others." Take for example the child who enjoys "clowning." In school, with his classmates, he is expected, or thinks he is expected, to be the class clown. When he is with the same people in other situations, he may continue to perform that role, feeling it is expected of him. Yet, when placed in a group of strangers, such as those at summer camp, he may reject the "clown role" for a more serious one. However, if some of his "critical others" friends come into the new group, he may immediately revert to his clown behavior, rejecting his new status and role expectations.

The way we carry out our *roles* varies according to our experiences and feedback. For example, the recent college graduate goes to work for a recreation department and although her position may be "down the line" in terms of organization structure, she assumes that it requires her to act differently than in the way she acted in her student days (student role). She may change her wardrobe, hair style, and social group affiliations. She wants to act like a professional. If she discovers, however, that the other full-time recreation employees do not have her concept of the professional (image and action), she may reject her ideas as idealistic and adopt their pattern. She does this to be accepted, to become one of the group.

Status is simply the position one holds in a group. Certain positions carry higher status. For example, being supervisor is more prestigious than being activity leader. Status usually reflects the number of persons holding a similar position; the more people in a given position, the lower the status of the position. Frequently, status is related to the skills required to carry out a certain role. If a position requires unusual skills, and if the position is critical to the function of the organization, those in that position have a higher status. Every group and every group member has status. Training, responsibility of possessing a given skill and public recognition are all essential to status.

With status comes role. *Role* is the performing of one's position; it is the acting of one's status. Each of us has our perception of the way we are to perform, and that is why there is such diversity in action. Being able to recognize the key positions in a group is essential to students of group dynamics. Also, understanding the role expectations and role performance of each position is critical. For example, what is the status of recreation therapy in a psychiatric hospital? What role do other mental health personnel (doctors, nurses, occupational therapists), expect of recreation, of the recreation therapist? The answers to these and similar questions about status can determine, to a great degree the success of the recreator in that situation. It certainly determines the role he is allowed to play. Prior experiences, one's value system, membership in a particular social class, and training, shape role expectation and role performance.

The EIAG Model

The *EIAG Model* is a useful tool in the study of group dynamics. It stimulates the individual to internalize what a certain activity or event means to him or her. EIAG is an acronym for *Experience, Identify, Analyze,* and *Generalize.* In all group interactions, there is an *experience.* From that experience, one can *identify* what variables made up that experience. Next it is possible to *analyze* which variables made it a positive or a negative experience and why. Finally it is possible to *generalize* about that experience. The EIAG Model enables individuals to identify the flaws in their group's functioning, or the reasons why the experience was either a success or a failure. Participants should complete Exercise 1; then distribute *Handout A* to participants to list the components of the EIAG model.

Listening–A Dynamic Activity

Listening takes both concentration and effort. The average American can speak about 125 words per minute, but can think at a rate of 500 words per minute. Without working at it, a listener can get lost during the 375 words per minute differential. Listening is an art and a skill and is essential for efficient and effective group functioning.

Listening involves six distinct active steps:

1. Be There! Be present in heart, mind and spirit in relationship with the speaker.
2. Accept this person without judgment or reservation.
3. Keep out of it, remain objective and refrain from intruding physically, verbally or mentally.
4. Accept the responsibility that goes along with what is or has been shared with you.
5. Don't plan what you are going to say. Focus in on listening to what is being said rather than debating how to solve, how to admonish, how to advise, or how to solace.

6. Understand what is being felt as well as what is being said. Listen to *intent* as well as *content*.

Exercise 2, as well as *Handouts B*, and *C* correspond to the listening material.

Feelings as Basic Motivators of Human Behavior

How we feel about a certain situation, issue, cause or subject determines how we will act. Feelings are the primary motivators that spur us to behave in different ways. An individual's feelings can also significantly stimulate, or conversely, restrict group functioning. An understanding of the relationship between feelings, motivation, and behavior is paramount to the success of any group. The spectrum of feelings an individual can tap into is vast indeed. However, these feelings can be grouped into the following eight categories: happy, afraid, hurt, angry, interested, fearless, eager, and doubtful. Have the participants complete Exercise 3 to reinforce the impact of feelings on the effectiveness of groups.

Levels of Group Functioning

All social groups share a similar history pattern of behavior regardless of their reason for being. They progress through various stages of action and share common elements of structure. Because each stage and element has its own characteristic and purpose and all are important to the health of the group, students of group dynamics need to be aware of them. Essentially the stages or levels of functioning are *stroking*, *organizing*, *producing*, and *creating*.

Stroking

When people get together, the first thing they do in a group situation is stroke. Stroking is nothing more than exchanging social amenities. It may take the form of kidding, shaking hands, smiling, or doing anything that sends the message: "I recognize you and it's good to see you again." The more familiar members are with each other, the more time they devote to stroking. New groups often seem cold and indifferent because members have not developed enough commitment to each other to stroke. The stroking period is formal and minimal. Well-established groups need lots of stroking time. It is important to allow for it.

Organizing

Every group has some form of organization and structure. Its rules of behavior may be conscious or unconscious, but its members are aware of them. Since leadership is a shared responsibility, certain members of the group may spend more time working on the group's organizational activities than other members. They are concerned with procedures and structures. They understand that organization is basic to production. When the group's need for stroking is filled, someone gets it moving with organizational statements like "Okay, lets get down to business." Groups may be formally organized with by-laws and officers who carry out its procedures, or they may function on some loosely structured, informal process. In either case, groups must organize in order to act.

Producing

Producing is doing. It is what happens when a group moves toward fulfilling its objectives. When the panel members are debating a point, they are producing. When the team scores points, it is producing. When a staff makes decisions, it is producing. Production takes many forms, and it is both the process of achieving as well as the achievement itself. For groups to continue, they must have a sense of movement, and that is producing.

Creating

Some groups are creative. They have little difficulty in moving toward this level of performance, an extension of producing. When groups are creative, they are usually unaware of time and space. They are caught up in the experience and are totally involved in it. To some degree, the statement "Where did the time go? It seems like we only got started, then suddenly it was time to leave" best characterizes the creative experience. For some, achieving creativity is the highest form of the recreative experience. Of course, some groups never achieve this level of production, yet they remain as groups. Creativity is not a prerequisite for group maintenance, but it goes a long way in keeping a group vital and fulfilled.

Although we have described these levels of functioning as a series of steps, they need not always be ascending in order. They are dynamic, and groups move from one level to another, back and forth, just as a child playing on steps may skip from one to the other and back again. Frequently groups, especially in their producing stage, become very tense. Conflicts may develop; when they do, they may be handled by dropping back to a level of stroking (joking) or organizing. Someone may make a kidding remark, the group laughs, and then it is ready to go back to work. The working stage (producing) is again introduced by someone who makes an organizational statement or action that gives it direction.

Some groups get locked into one level and have difficulty moving to the next. When this occurs, the recreator needs to assess why the group is meeting and why it has become static—spending all of its time on stroking or organizing. For example, if a teenage club is having difficulty maintaining interest in its club meetings—its members would rather spend time joking and kidding with each other (stroking) than doing the meeting task assigned it—then the meaning of the meeting should be questioned. Are the tasks relevant? Has proper organizational structure been developed to move the group from its stroking to task (producing) levels? Maybe there are differences between the goals of the club officers and recreation specialist (club advisor) and those of the members. The members may feel left out of the decision making process and consequently use the club meeting time as time for "fooling around." By carefully analyzing where the group is and what it is doing, proper action can be taken to make it dynamic again. Skill in recognizing this and acting to help the group produce are what recreation and park professionals must develop to be effective leaders.

The shifts from one level of function to another are similar to the shifts that occur when driving an automobile with automatic transmission. When the car slows down or extra power is needed, the transmission automatically moves to a lower gear. When extra power is no longer needed, it shifts to another level. The same is true for groups.

Group Properties

A universal set of characteristics of the group are its properties. Regardless of the group's structure, complexity, or purpose, all groups possess these properties. They have their *purpose*, their *procedures*, their *patterns of communication*, their *organizational structure*, their *cohesiveness*, their *patterns of interaction*, their *tone* or *social atmosphere*, their *degree of internal commitment*, and their *history*.

Purpose

For a group to exist, there must be a purpose that meets the needs of its members, or the group will cease to function as a group. Some groups formally state their goals or purpose, such as the recreation department goal "to provide recreation opportunities for the citizens of a community." Others, like the family, have implied goals, such as the continuation of the species, the educating of the young, and/or the protecting of the group from others or from natural disasters. Group goals may be verbalized or unspoken (simply understood), but in all instances they are necessary to the group's functioning. In the recreation setting, it has been observed that when group members understand the group's purpose and clearly state the group's goals, they tend to have a better tone and a high probability of reaching their objectives.

Tone or Social Atmosphere

Groups give out "vibes" just as do individuals. When group members are in harmony, the tone or social atmosphere is one of warmth, freedom, and conviviality. It is best illustrated in the following manner: When you walk into a room where people are enjoying themselves and are at ease, you feel the climate. On the other hand, when groups are tense, threatened, or anticipating conflict, the social atmosphere is quite different. They tend to be hostile, formal and restrained. Like taking one's temperature, an observer can read the tone of the group by sensing its atmosphere. The more positive the atmosphere, the more productive the group.

Cohesion

To a great extent social tone of the group is directly related to the commitment individual members make to each other and to the group. If there is a sense of team work, of commitment and a "we feeling," then the atmosphere is going to be positive, even when the group is experiencing conflict. Cliques, factions, and egocentric individuals erode the group's spirit and negatively affect its ability to pull together. When they are present, there is little group cohesion. One of the best indicators of group cohesiveness is the members' reference to themselves as a group, such as "OUR GANG," "MY TEAM," "OUR STAFF."

Organizational Structure

Every group has both a formal and informal organizational structure. There are acknowledged leaders or positions of responsibility, and tasks are delegated to those who hold these positions. These are formal leaders in the formal structure. Some organizations are quite complex with various levels of responsibility, while others are simplistic. For example, the formal structure of the recreation department may take a pyramidal form with the director at the top and the activities at the base. Between these two may be several levels of authority and a variety of subgroups (departments) with varying structures. On the other hand, the formal structure may be as obvious as the baseball manager and his players. The informal structure reflects the interaction between leaders and followers. In it group members know to whom to go to get certain jobs done regardless of their position or formal duties. In some groups the two, formal and informal, are one and the same. The group's power structure and communication patterns are intertwined with the organizational structure.

Patterns of Communication

To facilitate group functioning, a communications network of "sending and receiving" messages is established. It takes many forms, such as specialized vocabulary or jargon, body language and facial expressions, particularly among key group members, and the establishment of network focal points. We learn to whom we should listen, whom to ignore, which messages are important, and which ones are "window dressings." Problems develop when communication links break down and we act on what we *think* is being said rather than what is being said. Successful groups develop good feedback mechanisms and a well-defined network of information exchange.

Patterns of Interaction

Closely related to communications is the group's pattern of interaction. In time, there develops an expected pattern of communications and responses, a particular sequence of who speaks, after whom, to whom, and when. For example, when A speaks, B and C respond, but when C speaks, no one responds. Patterns of interaction vary according to many factors, such as the seniority and status (position) of the speaker (research shows that leaders tend to speak to the group as a unit, whereas followers tend to speak to specific individuals), the length of time the group has been together, and its tone. Patterns of interaction can be charted; these charts can help in determining the key communication linkage and decision-makers. Sociometric patterns and interaction patterns are closely related.

Procedures

Every group develops its way of getting things done. The range is from a highly structured obedience to *Robert's Rules of Order* with a set agenda and order of business to an informal pattern of dealing with issues as they develop according to the feelings of the group. What is essential is the members' recognition that some procedure for getting things done is necessary and that groups do modify their procedures as they develop their structures, interaction patterns, and history.

As groups develop procedures, standards are established. How things are done becomes as important as what is done. Certain subjects and actions may be taboo while others are encouraged. In many ways procedures and standards are the group rules by which the group game is played. Irritation, frustration, and inaction occur when these rules are not understood or are disregarded by members "who should know better." The choice of procedure is directly related to the group's history, the issues involved, the nature of the group and its meeting, and the styles of its leadership.

Internal Commitment

It is axiomatic that the more involved the members of a group are in determining their goals and direction, the more committed they are to carrying them out. Since the degrees of personal investment may vary from goal to goal, the degree of commitment members have to the group varies according to the issues involved. Fluctuations in commitment occur both within the group as a unit and within individual members. It is difficult to get excited about very long-range goals. Those which demand immediate action tend to get our attention and commitment. That is why it is important for groups to have a set of intermediate tasks that sustain interest while the group moves toward the accomplishment of its long-range objectives. A favorable social climate and communications pattern can strengthen the commitment of members to the group in general, even when their commitment to a specific program is not great.

Group History

Groups are comprised of individuals with a history of group experiences. Each group also has a history of its own experience as a group. These two facts play critical roles in determining the success of any group endeavor. When the program administrator meets with his or her advisory board for the first time, it may not be the first time the advisory board has met with a program director. The history of their past experiences sets for them their expectations–they want the director to act in a certain way and expect a procedure much like that followed in the past. Similarly, the program director comes to the meeting with a personal bias, based upon previous experiences with program commissions and advisory boards.

The success of the relationship between the two parties may hinge critically upon their ability to overcome their past history and develop a history unique to their relationship.

The more frequently a group meets, the better acquainted the members become with each other, expecting certain roles and functions to be performed. Members take on certain behaviors and patterns of interaction, not all of which are positive. Consequently, they may misuse their opportunities and time without recognizing what is happening. They have become accustomed to "poor" performance. It is healthy for a group periodically to pause and reflect upon its past and its present behavior to see if it is consistent with its ideals, particularly as its past relates to its present performance. Participants should complete Exercise 4 to understand the various roles of observation together with patterns of communication.

Essential Group Roles

Certain general roles are evident in all groups. These general roles can be classified according to function in terms of group building and maintenance roles and group task function roles.

Group building, maintenance roles, and/or *task functions* are important for ensuring the fulfillment of individual and personal needs. Essentially there are five group building and maintenance functions. These include tone setting, harmonizing, gatekeeping, standard setting and tension reducing.

- *Tone setting* encourages unthreatened member participation.
- *Harmonizing* is a mediating and conciliatory function for resolving internal disputes.
- *Gatekeeping* is a way of facilitating contributions from all group members.
- *Standard setting* involves the enforcement of agreed-upon roles of conduct and ethical standards.
- *Tension reducing* encourages stroking to reduce negative feelings, through the presentation of positive points of view.

Task Function Roles are necessary to ensure achievement of group goals. There are seven different task functions:

- *Opinion seeking* and *giving* involves asking for members' opinions and providing feedback.
- *Information seeking* and *giving* is the relaying of relevant information necessary for group tasks.

- *Clarifying* and *elaborating* involves building upon previous comments and focusing on key information.
- *Coordinating* is the channeling of ideas into a unified, demonstrable relationship.
- *Testing* is checking with the group to see if an action or decision is ready to be made.
- *Initiating* requires introducing new concepts or discussing the actions to be taken toward achieving group goals.
- *Summarizing* is the synthesizing of pertinent information and verbalizing the consensus decision made by the group.

All of the above roles are essential to group success. An effective group will have at least one member who plays each of these roles.

Negative Group Roles

Not all group roles are positive in nature. When an individual joins a group out of selfish motivation, it may have a serious effect on group morale and/or group functioning. There are primarily five different negative roles.

- *Aggressive behavior* refers to hostility shown by one group member to others in the group. This may take the form of criticizing, blaming or verbal attacks.
- *Blocking* refers to the impeding of the decision-making process through irrelevant digressions, pointless arguing or other like diversions.
- *Special interest pleading* occurs when a group member seeks special consideration for personal ideas and projects.
- *Withdrawing* refers to apathetic and disinterested behavior assumed by a group member. Such behaviors include, becoming indifferent and passive, doodling, remaining silent or engaging in side conversations.
- *Clowning* refers to individual attention-seeking which hampers group functioning.

Group Membership Roles

Each individual group member can assume a number of different group membership roles. Let's look at 17 of these roles:

- Model Member–Considers the needs of the group and its goals (this member is rare).

- Eager Beaver–Values efficiency and speed above deliberation and careful thinking.
- Talker–Enjoys talking, is interested in reaching a satisfactory conclusion, and feels that his material is necessary for that conclusion.
- Brilliant One–Extremely intelligent; often proposes the only solution and remains silent if his solution is not accepted.
- Emotional One–Reacts passionately to the contributions of others, either negatively or positively.
- Bored One–Sees discussion as a waste of time and would rather be somewhere else.
- Silent One–Chooses not to contribute due to shyness or the belief that he has nothing worth contributing.
- Conformist–Agrees with all that is said and avoids disagreements.
- Recognition Seeker–Ambitious and capable, this type constantly attempts to bring attention to himself.
- Playboy, Playgirl–Regards all meetings as social occasions, choosing to leave serious thinking to others.
- Suspicious One–Paranoid in the belief that everyone is motivated by selfish interests and will agree only on points by which they will profit personally.
- Nonconformist–Strongly dislikes being a member of the majority and enjoys defending a position against the rest of the group.
- Challenger–Seeks disagreement, opposing the leader as a matter of principle.
- Aggressive One–Regards any discussion as a fight.
- Debunker–Has nothing to contribute and denies the possibility that anyone else does either.
- Social Pleader–Attends discussion out of self-interest.
- Blocker–Major interest is in preventing the group from fulfilling its goals, believing the group to be irresponsible and stupid.

Internal and External Forces

There are both internal and external forces that affect the dynamics of the group as a whole. External forces tend to be part of the physical atmosphere that surrounds the group. Some examples of external dynamics might include the following: Space in which the group meets, time period and agenda, lighting and acoustics, comfort of the seating, availability of refreshments, restroom facilities, office supplies, temperature of the room, colors of the walls and related decor. These facility-related details are often overlooked when planning group meetings, but they can have a significant impact on the ultimate effectiveness of the group.

Internal forces are often divided into three clusters. Cluster-A forces are the highly visible dynamics such as group size, dress, attendance, sex, agenda content, and participation. Cluster-B forces are the less visible dynamics such as motivation, perceived status of various group members, definition of roles, atmosphere or emotional tone, energy flow, homogeneity of group interests, leadership style, norms and standards, participation patterns, group motives and aspirations, and the phases of group development or maturity of the group. Finally, Cluster-C forces are the intangibles such as feelings of the individual group members toward each other and the group, and the general openness or lack of openness of the group members.

External Forces

A considerable variety of forces external to the group affect the group as a whole. These external forces also affect the individual participant in ways which vary from person to person. All have some effect on the dynamics of the group as a whole. Some examples of external dynamics would be:

- The amount of time formally or informally allotted for the group to meet (begin at 8:00 p.m.; close no later than 10 p.m.) or the length of time devoted to each item on the agenda.
- The space in which the group meets.
- The amount of free space to move around.
- Lighting (is it sufficient for people to see each other?).
- Acoustics (can group members be heard by each other? Do sounds carry from outside the group?).
- Openness in the meeting area (are there pillars, compartments, or corners jutting into the room?).
- Seats (are they comfortable?).
- "The mind can absorb no more than the 'sitter' can endure!"
- Is the seating around a table or tables? Tables are helpful to lean on or write upon, but they are also a physical barrier. It is a research-based fact that furniture between persons is also a barrier between persons.
- Is there isolation of the group, either in a closed room or in an area free of interruptions?
- Do people pass through the room occasionally, or enter the room to get something or perhaps deliver some message?
- Is the isolation for extended periods of several days, or are there interruptions of phone calls, visits from family or friends, trips home or trips to sightsee, et cetera?

- If several meetings are in sequence, does the group recreate and eat together, or separately? Does the order in which things occur (the sequence of events within a meeting) affect the process?
- In the meeting room, are sufficient electrical outlets available? TV screens? TV equipment and extension cords? Paper and pencils? Tape, felt tip markers, et cetera?
- If smoking is planned, are there ashtrays for each smoker? Is there provision for smokers to leave the room if group consensus is opposed to smoking?
- Are refreshments available in the room?
- Are restrooms in close proximity, or located behind doors leading to the room?
- Will there be any observers who, though they do not participate in the meeting, can reduce trust and increase threat to openness of the group members?
- Is the temperature of the room consistent and comfortable to all members?
- Are the colors of the walls and other decor components attractive (yet non-distracting) and comfortable for the group members?
- Are the physical properties of the room surrounding the group attractive and neat, or are they distracting?

The effect of the external forces upon the individual members and upon the group as a whole is too often unrealized or overlooked. That these external forces can have a significant impact on the internal dynamics of the group could hardly be doubted after scanning the list of possible external forces listed above.

Internal Forces

Within the group also, a number of internal forces exist. Some or all of those that follow can profoundly affect the dynamics of the group as a whole and the individual members who contribute to the group's dynamics.

Internal dynamics are numerous in both cause and kind in relation to a group. Some are highly visible, such as group size, dress, attendance, sex, ages of group members, participation, skills in human relations, and agenda content for discussion or communication. We shall call these "*Cluster-A.*" Other internal dynamics are less visible and are more forces or energies. A person skilled in the process of groups can often "read" or "feel" or "sense" a number of these less visible internal dynamics and put them to good use. The more knowledgeable you are of the individual members of the group, the more your skills are compounded in effective "reading" and use of these dynamics for the good of the group.

Some of the less visible or invisible dynamics that affect the ongoing nature of the group and communications within the group would include motivation, perceived status of various group members, definition of roles, atmosphere or emotional tone, energy flow, heterogeneity, or homogeneity of the group interests, and leadership style. Others are the group's cohesiveness, norms and standards, participation patterns, relation to other groups in the system of which this group is a part, and the phases of group development or maturity of the group. Still others are identity of individuals and of the group as a whole, the power and influence of the group and group members, internal pressure to conform, group motives and aspirations and the desire of individual members to achieve. We shall call these less visible forces "*Cluster B.*" "*Cluster C*" is composed of feelings, the feelings of the individual group members toward each other and the group, and the general openness or lack of openness of the group members.

What to Look For in Groups

A number of different observational guidelines can be used to help analyze group behavior. These guidelines can be grouped into the following categories: Participation, style of influence, decision-making procedures, task functions, maintenance functions, group atmosphere, membership, feelings and norms.

Participation—One indication of involvement is verbal participation. It can be useful to look for differences in the amount of participation among members. Who are the high and low participators? Who talks to whom? How are the silent people treated? Which members have high and low influence? Is there rivalry or a struggle for leadership?

Style of influence—Influence can take many forms and can be both positive and negative. It can enlist the support or cooperation of others or alienate them. How a person attempts to influence another may be the crucial factor in determining how open or closed the other will be toward being influenced. There are four leadership styles worthy of note:

- *Autocratic*—These are individuals who attempt to impose their will, judgment and values on others.
- *Peacemaker*—These are individuals who support and empower other group members.
- *Laissez-Faire*—These are individuals who display total lack of involvement and who are withdrawn, uninvolved, and uncommitted.

- *Democratic*–These are individuals who express feelings openly, directly and honestly and who try to include everybody in the discussion.

Decision-making procedures–Many kinds of decisions are made in groups without considering the effects of those decisions on other group members. Some questions to consider might include: Does anyone make a decision and carry it out without checking with other group members? Does the group drift from one topic to another? Who supports other members' suggestions or decisions? Is there any attempt to engage a consensus?

The level of group agreement affects the feelings various group members have when decisions are being made. This group feeling is called *inner group harmony. Disharmony* is evidenced by lack of cooperation, member drop-out, and low group participation.

Happy members are characterized by those who have certain needs answered. Group members need a sense of belonging, a share in planning the group goals, a share in making the rules, to know what is expected, to have challenging responsibilities, to see that progress is being made, and to have confidence and trust in the leader.

Task functions–These functions illustrate behaviors that are concerned with getting the job done, or accomplishing the task that the group has before them. For instance: Who keeps the group on target? Who provides opinions, information, feedback, summaries, et cetera?

Maintenance functions–These functions maintain a harmonious working relationship and atmosphere within a group, insuring smooth and effective teamwork. Guidelines here could include: Who are the gate openers and gate closers? How well are members getting their ideas across? How are ideas rejected and what are their consequences?

Group atmosphere–The way in which the group works as a unit creates a certain atmosphere. It is important to be aware of members who seem to prefer a congenial atmosphere and those who seem to prefer an atmosphere of conflict and disagreement. Also, do people seem involved and interested?

Membership–A major concern for group members is the degree of acceptance or inclusion in the group. Some questions to consider might include: Is there any sub-grouping or "cliquing"? Which people seem to be watching from outside the group, and which seem to be "in" in the group? Do some members move in and out of the group?

Feelings–During most group discussion, feelings are frequently stimulated by the interactions between members. Observers may have to make guesses about members' feelings based on tone of voice, facial expressions, gestures, and the many other forms of nonverbal cues.

Norms–Standards or ground rules frequently develop in a group that controls the behavior of its members. These ground rules are referred to as *norms*. Norms usually express the beliefs or desires of the majority of the group members as to what behaviors should or should not take place in the group. Some norms facilitate group progress, while others hinder it. In regards to group norms, some questions to consider might include: Are certain subjects avoided in the group? Are group members overly nice or polite to each other? Are only positive feelings expressed? Do members feel free to probe each other about their feelings?

Use *Handouts D* and *E* with this material.

Conflict Resolution

Negative kinds of conflict include blame, avoidance, denial, placating, irrelevancy, and negative power. However, there are positive kinds of conflict resolution which come from positive power moves, rational approaches and creative interchange.

Conflict generally occurs for three different reasons when people interact in a group setting. One of these is that the group has a common task, but each member suggests different approaches or ideas. Another is that the group has the same needs, but they don't have enough resources to meet all of their needs. The third reason conflict may occur in a group is that the group has divergent needs, values or goals.

Conflict has tremendous energy and should be viewed positively. Harnessing this energy can lead to constructive resolution of the conflict in ways which will bring benefit, or a sense of success and accomplishment, to most (if not all) parties involved. Use Exercise 5 and *Handouts F* and *G* to give the participant some ideas for using conflict to the group's advantage.

Creative Interchange

Creative interchange is the ability whereby individuals can deal constructively with conflict. Creative interchange is broken down into four different processes: interacting, appreciating, integrating and expanding.

The conditions that must be available for facilitating the process of *Interacting* include trust, spontaneity, and honesty. The results include an increased knowledge, increased individual uniqueness, and diversity of thoughts, feelings, values, behavior, motives, needs, and perspectives.

The conditions that must be available for facilitating the process of *Appreciating* include awareness, understanding, and accepting. The result is increased value.

The conditions that must be available for facilitating the process of *Integrating* include openness, synergy, and actualization. The results include an increased control, increased identity and wholeness, and increased freedom.

The conditions that must be available for facilitating the process of *Expanding* include interdependence, intimacy, and commitment. The results include an increased community, increased cooperation, and increased cohesiveness.

After completing this section, *Transparency 1* can be used to summarize the entire *Group Dynamics* chapter. Exercise 6 may then be completed following the summary.

INSTRUCTOR NOTES–OVERVIEW

Due to the large number of exercises accompanying this chapter, we have provided this overview, which explains each activity. Instructors should explain the exercises to the participants verbally. Participants do not need copies of the exercise explanations unless the instructor thinks it is necessary. They need only to receive copies of the handouts that accompany the specific exercises and those referred to within the text of the chapter.

Exercise 1: This is an exercise designed to show that participation by everyone is desirable and that participants will gain much more if they are willing to take the risk and get involved.

Exercise 2: This exercise should complement the discussion on listening as a dynamic activity. After the exercise, time should be given for participants to discuss how effectively they were communicating with one another.

Exercise 3: This exercise is designed to show the importance of feelings as basic motivations for human behavior. Every effort should be made to encourage different group members to volunteer in the conducting of the exercise as well as the feedback.

Exercise 4: This exercise is designed to help participants understand the various roles of observation together with patterns of communication.

Exercise 5: This exercise should demonstrate the importance of being able to work as a group to solve a problem. This should also stimulate a discussion on conflict and means of dealing with conflict.

Exercise 6: This is an exercise designed to reinforce what the group has learned over the course of the training session. This exercise should provide access to the various flip chart pages used throughout the session as ideas.

Handout A which shows the EIAG Model should be explained. Participants should be made aware that after each experience the group will identify what was done in the experience, analyze what was experienced, and generalize what was learned from the experience.

Handout B and *C*: These handouts should complement the discussion stimulated through the initiation of Exercise 2.

Handout D is a guide as to what will help group decision-making.

Handout E: This inventory should allow the individual to examine his or her feelings about themselves and their participation in groups. The purpose of this exercise is to aid in continuing the development of group skills.

Handout F explains strategies for positive conflict resolution and *Handout G* explains the concept of creative interchange.

Group Dynamics

Exercises, Handouts and Transparencies

Exercise 1: Concept of Risk versus Gain

In this exercise a line should be drawn on the board with a magic marker with 0 at one end and 100 at the other. The word GAIN printed in capital letters should be then written above it. The group is then asked how much they are willing to gain, and how much they would like to gain from participating in the training program. Most people will say somewhere between 50 and 100. The cluster is usually between 90 and 100 percent.

Next, another line should be drawn with the 0 and 100 marks with the word RISK written above it. Now the group is asked how much they would be willing to risk in order to gain from the workshop. The general response is that most people are willing to risk as much as they would like to gain. The instructor should indicate to the participants that participation by everyone is desirable and that they will gain much more if they are all willing to take the risk and get involved.

Exercise 2: Listening as a Dynamic Activity

In this exercise all participants are asked to choose a partner (these are "sharing pairs"). Partners will periodically be changed over the course of

HANDOUT A

The EIAG Model for Experience Based Learning

EXPERIENCE - Do It

IDENTIFY - Look At It

ANALYZE - Think About It

GENERALIZE - What You Have Learned

the exercise. In each pair one person becomes "A" and the other "B." In these discussions the instructor should suggest the topics and allow for 45 seconds for each person to discuss that topic with their partner. In the first round, the first person might discuss a favorite teacher from high school or college and describe that person and why that person was a favorite. Having done this by some predetermined manner, the instructor should stop the discussion and ask the first person to raise his/her hand and the second to go find another partner. When the people have all changed partners the instructor should assign another topic such as a favorite place in North America. The instructor should allow participants to exchange several times, always changing topic. Other topics possibilities might include: favorite food, a favorite birthday experience, a favorite outdoor place, a favorite teacher, or a person who has had the most influence on the participant's life.

When the exercise is over, the group should be asked to move into a semi-circle facing the flip chart. A discussion should be encouraged asking participants to discuss how they could tell that the people with whom they were talking understood the meaning of what they were trying to say. At this point the instructor can refer to *Handouts B* and *C*. The instructor should explain that we can speak about 125 words a minute, that we can listen to 500 words per minute, and that we can think up to 12,500 words a minute. One of the reasons people do not listen well is that they do not pay attention. They assume where the other person is leading the conversation, and they begin to think about some kind of other response that they are going to make when the person stops talking. The instructor should next inform participants that 7% of communication is words, 35% is sound, and 58% is nonverbal.

For an understanding of communication, one must also clearly comprehend the process of listening. Communication begins at the source of what one wants to say. It becomes the mind's visual image one's favorite place, meal, person or birthday, for example. One then expresses the image in some message form. In this country, the English language is the code. There is a channel which represents the totality of one's being. This channel represents the verbal and nonverbal signals, hand movements, eyes, voice, intensity of speaking and all that one has to present the message to the receiver. The instructor should refer back to the sharing pairs activity. Participants should be asked whether they were communicating effectively. A good receiver constantly sends feedback to the sender so that the sender will know whether or not he/she is getting through.

Exercise 3: Feelings as Motivators of Human Behavior

In this exercise the instructor should solicit the help of six volunteers. On six pieces of paper the following words should be written in large capital letters: Fear, Anger, Love, Rejection, Embarrassment, and Guilt. Each volunteer should be told to choose a piece of paper while the instructor holds them out, turned face down and fanned out, like a deck of cards. Next each participant should be instructed to talk for about a minute and say:

- What their word is,
- What their name is or where they are from,
- Describe a time or experience in their lives when that word has been at an intense or strong level for them.

After each of the six people have shared their experiences participants should be instructed as to the importance of feelings and how they are a major motivator of human behavior. Most people try to conduct themselves or live their lives or behave in ways which will promote good feelings, such as confidence, success, accomplishment, appreciation and recognition. They try to avoid such things as embarrassment, rejection or failure or other such negative feelings. In a group, people should be aware

HANDOUT B

Listening—A Dynamic Activity

Listening takes concentration and effort. The average American can speak about 125 words per minute, but can <u>think</u> some 500 words per minute. Without working at it, a listener can get lost or let his/her mind wander during the 375 words per minute differential!

Listening is an art, a skill which can be developed. Few have this skill naturally, since over 150 Ph.D. dissertations have been written about listening to help <u>improve</u> our skills! It is an act which we can and must practice if effective communication (if real dialogue or "meeting or meaning") is to take place.

Berlo's Source-Message-Channel-Receiver device requires the Receiver to listen <u>actively.</u> We need to listen, therefore with the "Third Ear," processing data from eyes and ears, non-verbal as well as verbal. Some helpful ideas for listening in a group is below left, and for listening one-to-one below right. Both can help.

Listening in a Group
1. Stop talking!
2. Establish agreeable atmosphere.
3. Look for areas of interest.
4. Judge content, not delivery.
5. Remove distractions.
6. Empathize with sender.
7. Be patient.
8. Listen for central ideas.
9. Be flexible in note taking.
10. Hold your temper.
11. Go easy on criticism.
12. Keep your mind open.
13. Ask questions.
14. Restate for feedback and accuracy.
15. Listen for feelings plus meaning.

Listening to Understand Another
Listening is a very active, muscular experience. It involves 6 distinct active steps:

1. Be there! Be present in heart, mind, and spirit in relationship with this person.

2. Accept this person as he or she is wholly and without judgment or reservation or putting the person in a mental box or category.

3. Keep out of it, keep yourself removed, stay objective. Don't intrude physically, verbally, or mentally. Be quiet. Listen. This is difficult and <u>not</u> passive.

4. Accept the responsibility for walking gently through some of the tender, personal areas of another person's life as shared with you.

5. Listen. Don't plan what you are going to say. Don't think you can interrupt if you are just quick enough about it. Don't think how to solve, how to admonish, how to advise, how to solace.
<u>Don't think...listen!</u>

6. Understand what is being felt as well as what is being said. Hear every nuance of tone and meaning. Listen to intent and content. Listen. Put yourself in his or her shoes, his or her state of understanding.

HANDOUT C

Active Listening

When I listen actively, I:
- --respect the other person as having worth and value.
- --put aside my own views, opinions, judgments, and focus on the conversation.
- --look for nonverbal clues: tone of voice, eyes and other facial expressions and other body language (leg and hand movements, etc.).
- --am on the alert for feelings expressed and emotions behind the words.
- --recognize that feelings are neither "right" or "wrong" but are real and legitimate.
- --avoid thinking ahead as to how I'll respond to the other's comments.
- --avoid responding with my own message by giving advice and opinions; avoid imposing my expectations and values; do not judge, order or analyze.
- --become a "mirror" to reflect back what I understand the other person is saying--what meaning I get from his/her statements.
- --am comfortable with silence--feel no need to fill the void with talk.
- --am performing the most caring task I can "being there" for and with another person in his/her pain, sorrow, discomfort or joy.

As I listen creatively, I help another person:

- --become free and open with his/her feelings.
- --become less afraid of negative feelings.
- --"own" his/her particular problem(s).
- --work toward solving his/her own problem(s).
- --come to a fuller understanding of the shared relationship between persons.

of communication patterns *and* feelings. The instructor should comment on these things in an appropriate way.

Exercise 4: Observation and Patterns of Communication

In this exercise participants are divided into two equal groups and each told to select a topic for group discussion. Group A and Group B are asked to select two different topics for discussion as well as two leaders who will start the discussion for their group. Ten to 15 minutes should be allowed for the groups to discuss what topic they would be willing to discuss for 20 minutes in a circle. Participants should be made to understand that they will be in a small, fairly tight circle of chairs with nothing in the middle. They will also be surrounded by members of the other group sitting on the outside observing the discussion.

When ready the first group should be instructed to begin its discussion. It is important that the instructor be able to observe the group and write down in detail everything that is said by the group during the discussion. It is also important to indicate where there are smiles, laughter, harsh responses, ignoring of others' comments, et cetera. The instructor needs to point out behavior which could help others' by citing when an interruption or laughter came along, the time that it came, and the specific content of the comment from the group which preceded or followed the incident. This will help the participants to learn how to observe.

Efforts should be made to ensure that members of the observing group understand their various roles and have specific topic areas to explore. The instructor should assign participation, leadership roles, decision making, communication styles, sensitivity, and openness to different members of the observation group. If numbers are large, duplication of assignments is acceptable.

In addition, the instructor should ask two people to draw a sociogram on a circle about 7″ in diameter. A small circle should be drawn for each person participating in the discussion with their name assigned to it. The two chosen observers should be instructed to draw a line from the individual to the center of the circle if he/she speaks to the group as a whole, or to an individual circle if the comment is specifically directed. This nonverbal form of feedback on participation will enable the group to visualize participation styles.

The observing group should be allowed at least 15 minutes to provide verbal feedback on the process of the first group's discussion. The feedback should, where possible, cite phrases and/or quotations as examples. After discussing feedback the instructor may choose to instruct the groups to reverse the process so that observers discuss and discussants observe.

Often it is useful to complete a personal inventory on individual and group skills. This inventory, *Handout E,* can help provide a realistic picture of your feelings about yourself and your participation in groups.

Exercise 5: Moving Chairs

In this exercise, participants are divided into two groups of 10 volunteers with the remaining participants observing. The groups should then be differentiated from one another. One means of doing this is to place masking tape on the shoulder of one of the teams. The tape group is then sent out of the room with an instructor. This group is then given a sheet of paper explaining their task to them, "without speaking verbally the task of your group is to arrange the people from the other group and the chairs in a circle. When you shall have completed your task one person from the other group will be seated in each chair and one person from your group will be standing behind each chair with your hands on the shoulders of the person from the group in the chair in front of you. DO NOT SPEAK AT ALL until after the exercise is completed. You will have

HANDOUT D

What Will Help Group Decision-Making?

Group harmony, happy members, open discussion about why the decision must be made, a look at all sides and alternatives, a well-chosen decision making process, and a leader who cares but doesn't dominate. That's a tall order, but one that can be very rewarding.

Group Harmony

The level of group agreement affects the feelings various group members have when decisions are being made. The way a group feels after making a decision becomes important especially if the group plans to have a continuing positive relationship. The group has a feeling called "Inner Group" harmony.

Disharmony is evidenced by lack of group cooperation, members dropping the group, no new members being added, and low participation of those in the group

High levels of inner group harmony are noted by good feelings, people feeling as if they are needed in the group, high percentage of membership participation and shared decision making.

All groups (families, organizations, businesses, communities, etc.,) work best together when the harmony level is high.

Happy Members

Group members need:
* A Sense of Belonging—a feeling that no one objects to their presence, that they are welcome and needed.
* A Share in Planning the Group Goals—a feeling that their ideas are within reach, and a feeling that the group is doing something worthwhile.
* A Share in Making the Rules—the way the group will work together toward common goals.
* To Know What is Expected
* To Have Challenging responsibilities within their abilities and time limits.
* To See that Progress is Being made toward the group goals.
* To Have Confidence and Trust in the leader.

seven minutes after the signal is given to when this exercise must be completed." Meanwhile the other group is given similar instructions except they are told that without speaking verbally their task is to arrange all 10 chairs into two parallel lines, five on each side, with one other group member seated and one of their group standing behind each person in each chair. Both groups are reminded that winning happens only when their task is successfully completed at the end of seven minutes.

The instructor should be aware that this exercise creates not just minor, but

HANDOUT E

Inventory of Personal and Group Skills

Name_____Date_____

Purpose:

This inventory is designed to help you get a realistic picture of your feelings about yourself and your participation in groups. The only "right" answer is that which you feel genuinely describes yourself as you really are now. Do not pretend to be either better or worse. Try to discard any mask or "blinders." The purpose is to help you in your own development.

Instructions:

Read each item and decide how much this is true of you. Note that all ratings are numerical, to measure quantity, not quality. The questions ask for your estimate of the quantity of a function: How much is this like me? Seek to be accurate in your ratings. Use the complete scale, making use of the extreme ends of the scale as appropriate. Place a rating number before each question. Rate all questions.

1	2	3	4	5	6	7
Much less	Generally less	Slightly less	Average	Slightly more	Generally more	Much more

After completing all questions, review your answers. If there are any ratings where you feel there is a significant need for change, circle these ratings. Be selective, and do not circle more than three in each section.

Understanding and Disclosure of Myself

Self rating	How much is this like me?	Peer rating (how much is this like him?)
A		B C D
____	1. I am aware of what's going on inside me when I am interacting with others.	__ __ __
____	2. I feel "I'm O.K."	__ __ __
____	3. I clearly express myself with words.	__ __ __
____	4. I clearly express myself non-verbally.	__ __ __
____	5. I feel free to express a wide range of emotions.	__ __ __
____	6. I identify and express my feelings of anger and aggression.	__ __ __
____	7. I identify and meet my need for affection	__ __ __
____	8. I identify with and express my sexuality.	__ __ __
____	9. I try out new expressions and behavior.	__ __ __
____	10. I learn from disciplined reflection on immediate experience.	__ __ __

Understanding of and Response to Others in Groups

Self rating	How much is this like me?	Peer rating (how much is this like him?)		
A		B	C	D
____	1. I involve myself in the life of groups.	—	—	—
____	2. I recognize and accept differences in other people.	—	—	—
____	3. I accept selfhood in others: "You're O.K."	—	—	—
____	4. I listen with understanding of others' ideas and feelings.	—	—	—
____	5. I respond to the full range of verbal and nonverbal communication with others.	—	—	—
____	6. I show flexibility in adapting to changing situations.	—	—	—
____	7. I trust others in a group.	—	—	—
____	8. I confront and level with others in a group.	—	—	—
____	9. I am willing to share leadership.	—	—	—
____	10. I recognize and involve myself in expressions of anger and aggression with others.	—	—	—
____	11. I cope with conflict in groups.	—	—	—
____	12. I recognize and respond to affection shown by others	—	—	—
____	13. I recognize and respond to others.	—	—	—
____	14. I give feedback to others.	—	—	—
____	15. I receive and accept feedback from others.	—	—	—

major conflict. People are picked up and stuffed into chairs. They are pushed and pulled around the room, chairs are pushed and pulled. Investigate how it feels to be forced into a chair, to be pushed or held or to have a chair taken away. A discussion on effective group functioning should be encouraged as well as creative interchange as a means of conflict resolution (*Handouts E and F*).

Exercise 6: The "Wagon Wheel"

The purpose of this final exercise is to bring some closure and rein-forcement to the session. First of all, the participants should be instructed to list some of the things that they have gained as insights or new knowledge during

HANDOUT F

Disagreement/Conflict

Some strategies for solution

NEGATIVE STRATEGIES	POSITIVE STRATEGIES
Blame	Power (positive)
Avoidance	Rational
Denial	Creative Interchange
Placate	
Irrelevance	
Power (negative)	
These six all feel like	The best approach in
WIN/LOSE	conflict is a
Which usually leads to	**WIN/WIN**
LOSE/LOSE	strategy and feeling.

the course of the workshop. The instructor should make a list of as many things as the participants can recall and suggest they look around the room at the various flip chart pages placed on the walls to get ideas. A discussion of these insights by the participants of the workshop is called a "Wagon Wheel."

In the Wagon Wheel, the group is divided into subgroups of four. Each subgroup then picks one other group with whom to interact. The first subgroup is called the inner group and the second is called the outer group. The inner group puts their chairs back to back so that they are facing as on a clock moving out from 12, 3, 6, and 9. The outer group then pulls their chairs so each one is facing a member of the inner group. The instructor should allow about four minutes for each pair to talk to each other and two minutes for each one to share the things they have learned or the insights they have gotten. After four minutes the instructor should stop the entire process and ask the outer group to rotate one person to the left and then repeat the sharing process. When this is over, participants should rotate again, so each person learns from the other four

HANDOUT G

Creative Interchange

PROCESS	CONDITIONS FOR FACILITATING THE PROCESS	RESULTS
1. Interacting leads to ↓	1. **Trusting** (Willingness to risk) 2. **Spontaneity** (Here-and-Now self disclosure and feedback to others) 3. **Honesty** (Congruity of thought, feelings, values, behavior, etc.)	1. **Increased knowledge** 2. Increased individual uniqueness 3. Diversity of thoughts, feelings, values, behavior, motives, needs, perspectives
2. Appreciating leads to ↓	1. **Awareness** (Self, others, world) 2. **Understanding** (Empathy) 3. **Accepting** (No denial or devaluing)	1. **Increased value**
3. Integrating leads to ↓	1. **Openness** (Willingness to modify) (Unfreezing) 2. **Synergy** (Awareness of both–and) (Learning) 3. **Actualization** (Making new learning behavioral) (Refreezing)	1. **Increased control** (Coordination) 2. Increased identity & wholeness 3. Increased freedom
4. Expanding	1. **Interdependence** (Needs and resources of self and others) 2. **Intimacy** (Significant others and closeness) 3. **Commitment** (Loyalty to self, others, organization, and creative interchange)	1. **Increased Community** 2. Cooperation (Affection) 3. Cohesiveness

(N.B. Creative Interchange works best when both or all parties in conflict understand and Creative Interchange.)

Transparency 1

Group Dynamics
Key Points

1. The four stages that a group passes through are:

- stroking

- organizing

- creating

- producing

2. All groups have distinct properties. These include:

- purpose

- tone

- cohesion

- organizational structure

- patterns of communication

3. There are two types of groups—primary and secondary.

- An example of a primary group is your family.

- Secondary groups are social or work-related in nature.

4. Every group needs certain roles to be fulfilled.

- tone setting

- gatekeeping

- standard setting

- tension reducing

Transparency 1 (continued)

5. Some negative behaviors that impede group functioning include:

- aggressive behavior
- blocking
- special interest pleading
- withdrawing
- clowning

6. Both external (environmental) and internal (within the group) forces affect group functioning.

7. A person's values can determine the types of groups he seeks membership in.

8. An individual can assume many different kinds of roles when participating in a group.

9. Listening is a very active process and is essential to good group functioning.

10. The way a person is feeling at any given time can affect how he behaves in his group.

11. Conflict within a group should be viewed as a positive occurrence. There are many effective ways to resolve conflict in your group.

people and vice versa. Listening to others' experiences is by far the strongest possible reinforcement.

AUTHOR NOTE

The basic content of Chapter 11 comes from two sources: (1) *Leadership and Group Dynamics in Recreation Services* by H. Douglas Sessoms and Jack Lovett Stevenson, Reading, MA: Allyn and Bacon, Publisher, 1981; and (2) from workshop and seminar programs conducted by Jack Lovett Stevenson either while a professor at Clemson University from 1968-1991, or in programs conducted for national or southern corporations and organizations from 1976-1996 by Dr. Stevenson as president of his company, Creative Growth, Inc.

Most of the handouts are verbatim quotes taken directly from the Sessoms and Stevenson book noted above, or from graphics in Creative Growth's workbooks for seminars.

Chapter 12

Marketing

Sheila J. Backman

Learning Objective	Key Concepts/Terms	Instructor Notes
1. Introduce basic concept of marketing.	The evolution of marketing	Transparency 1 Transparency 2
2. Introduce the notion of exchange.	Customer wants/needs	Transparency 3
3. Focus on the company: What business are you in?	Investment (time and money); available resources	Exercise 1 Handout A
4. Introduce and explain the "4 Ps" of marketing.	Price; product; place; promotion	Transparency 4
5. Discuss why the "4 Ps" of product marketing are not appropriate for service marketing.	Programming; packaging; partnership; publicity	
6. Discuss the differences between product and service.	Tangibility; returnability; homogeneity; perishability marketing	Transparency 5
7. Discuss the importance of knowing customer wants.	Market intelligence; who, what, where, why and how of your customers	Transparency 6

[Haworth co-indexing entry note]: "Marketing." Backman, Sheila J. Co-published simultaneously in *Activities, Adaptation & Aging* (The Haworth Press, Inc.) Vol. 23, No. 3, 1999, pp. 171-188; and: *Preparing Participants for Intergenerational Interaction: Training for Success* (ed: Melissa O. Hawkins, Francis A. McGuire, and Kenneth F. Backman) The Haworth Press, Inc., 1999, pp. 163-179. Single or multiple copies of this article are available for a fee from The Haworth Document Delivery Service [1-800-342-9678, 9:00 a.m. - 5:00 p.m. (EST). E-mail address: getinfo@haworthpressinc.com].

8. Discuss the importance of developing new products and services.	Looking to the future; technology; environment and seasons	Transparency 7 Exercise 2, Handout B
9. Describe the process of market target identification.	Target markets; demographics; market segmentation	Transparency 8 Exercise 2, Handout B
10. Identify target markets for new products/services.	Exchange; benefits; identification of new products	Exercise 2, Handout B
11. Characterize the four stages in the Product Life Cycle (PLC).	Introduction; growth stage, maturity stage; decline stage	Transparency 10 Exercise 3, Handout C
12. Describe the process of retrenchment and how it can be used.	Retrenchment/termination; product withdrawal; PLC; persuade and remind	Transparency 9 Transparency 11 Exercise 3, Handout C
13. Describe the use of communication in product/service promotion.	Communication tools; advertising; personal selling; publicity; public relations; word of mouth	Transparency 12 Exercise 4, Handout D
14. Explain the basic elements of service quality.	Reliability; assurance; empathy	Exercise 5, Handout E
15. Describe the procedures for handling customer complaints.	Treat customers like people; be sincere; offer a solution; apologize; follow up	Transparency 13 Exercise 5, Handout E
16. Summarize key points.		Transparency 14

INTRODUCTION: MARKETING

The instructor should introduce him or herself, and welcome the participants. The instructor should discuss the reason for his/her presence as well as provide an introduction to marketing. The participants should be made aware that they will probably play a part in business at some point in their lives, and the role that they may play in delivering goods and services to customers is critical. Marketing aims at improving products and services, and delivering a quality product to the consumer. This session will help participants to improve their products, and help them gain a better understanding of what occurs during a business transaction.

It is recommended that the instructor administer several training sessions, with an optimum attendance of about 15 to 20 participants per session. Because the sessions are to be delivered to groups comprised of several different age levels, the trainer should be sensitive to the levels of knowledge, experience, and understanding that make up each group. Modifications can be made at the discretion of the instructor and are dependent upon the characteristics of the participants. This training is administered to provide the participants with an understanding of the fundamentals of business, and to facilitate creativity and cohesion within the groups.

IMPLEMENTATION AND MATERIALS SUGGESTIONS FOR THE INSTRUCTOR

This training session is ideally suited for about 30 participants. A classroom setting is best for delivering the material contained here; participants may arrange their desks in small clusters when small group discussion is called for. This session, depending on the length of discussions and time spent in groups, may last from two to three hours.

Supplies and Materials

Some things that you will or may need to conduct this training session include:

- overhead projector
- transparency markers
- extra transparencies
- copier (to make copies from handouts)
- flip chart or chalkboard
- pencils for use with the handouts

MARKETING

1. Basic Concepts and the Evolution of Marketing

"Marketing" connotes the selling of products and services, and thus should not be viewed as appropriate for non-profit or service organizations. On one hand, marketing is a philosophy, an attitude, and a perspective, and on the other, the set of activities used to implement that philosophy.

Marketing is the set of activities aimed at facilitating and expediting exchanges (see *Transparency 1*). It entails information collection, finding out what benefits customers want, identifying target markets, and developing the "marketing mix" (see *Transparency 2*).

Traditionally, marketing was seen as a process of trying to sell a product or service to people who may or may not desire or need the product. Marketing has evolved as it has passed through these stages: (a) product era, (b) sales era, and (c) marketing era. The marketing concept has moved from a primary focus on producing goods and services to a focus which emphasizes customer satisfaction. Marketing now is a continuous process which seeks to identify customers' needs prior to developing or promoting a product or service. It is important to note that this orientation focuses on knowing what the customer wants as opposed to simply selling what the company or organization has to sell. Companies which focus only on sales may achieve short-term goals, but generally lose in the long term to companies who keep customer needs and satisfaction first. A true marketing company starts with the needs of customers, then develops the products and follows with promotion.

2. The Principle of Exchange

The principle of exchange suggests that companies must have something of value for customers, and that customers have something to offer the companies in turn. Before customers purchase products, they ask the questions, "What's in it for me?" "How much will it cost?" "Does it benefit me?" If customers perceive that they will gain benefits, they will exchange money for the product. *Transparency 3* will be useful to demonstrate this principle to participants.

3. What Business Is Your Company in?

The most important question you must ask is, "What business are we in?" Customers invest time, money and energy in exchange for benefits; in other words, they purchase the expectation of benefits. The products themselves are not marketable; it is actually the benefits.

A company should define its business in terms of the benefits it offers customers, noting the product or service it sells. Companies should seek to answer the question: "What is the best way our company can provide customers with benefits, given our available resources?" *Exercise 1* and *Handout A* can be used to demonstrate some of these principles of defining your "business."

4. The "Four Ps" of Marketing

Product, Place, Price and Promotion are often referred to as the "Four Ps" of marketing. These four components work together to facilitate exchanges. Companies can manipulate the "Four Ps" to achieve desired outcomes.

Product is defined as the bundle of want-satisfying attributes. It is comprised of facilities and services that have been developed to deliver benefits to the target audience.

Place refers to the point at which the products are to be distributed. In many cases, the place is fixed.

Price refers to what a customer must give up to purchase the product. Both monetary and non-monetary costs should be considered. Non-monetary costs refer to the time and energy the customer invests in purchasing the product or service.

Promotion refers to transferring information from the company to its target markets. Typically the information refers to price, attributes of the product, and distribution information.

Transparency 4 outlines the "Four Ps" of marketing.

5. Why Are the "Four Ps" of Marketing Not Sufficient for Service Marketing?

Four additional "Ps," Programming, Packaging, Partnership and Publicity, have been added to the service "marketing mix." Programming refers to special events or activities designed to afford the customer the opportunity to use the service.

Packaging refers to combining a range of services and products into one package for one price.

Partnership refers to two organizations coming together to develop offspring, to share the costs of promotion. Organizations may work together to promote products, thus achieving cost savings.

Publicity will be discussed in Section 13, "Communication and Promotion."

6. The Differences Between Product and Service Marketing

Services differ from products in several ways. The key distinction between products and services is that services cannot be seen; they are intangible. Products, on the other hand, are tangible. A second distinction between the two focuses on the points of manufacture and consumption. Products are manufactured and consumed at two different locations. In contrast, services are manufactured and consumed at the point of distribution.

Another characteristic which distinguishes products from services is returnability. Products can be returned, however services cannot. Services are also perishable; they will expire if not used. Services cannot be inventoried and held for later sale. Finally, services differ from products because it is very difficult to deliver the same service each time.

Transparency 5 is to be used with this section in the training session.

7. Know Your Customers

There are many ways to get to know who your customers are. Segments can be developed on the basis of a number of variables. These include geographics, demographics, product and service usage, and psychographics.

Geographic descriptors such as zip codes, city size, and county of residence can be used to describe where customers live.

Demographic descriptors refer to age, gender, family size, life cycle stage, occupation and income. These variables are used to profile individuals and households.

Typical product and service usage variables include frequency of purchase, benefits sought, loyalty and purchase behavior. These variables describe the customer's use of a product or service.

Depending on the product or service, more than one set of these variables is used to segment markets.

Use *Transparency 6* to discuss the customer with participants.

8. Developing New Products and Services

All companies must continually seek to develop new products and services. Product and service ideas can emanate from many sources.

Your first step in developing a new product or service is to look to the future. Examine the impact that changing customer wants will have on your organization. Can the organization develop new products and services to meet these new wants?

Second, examine the environment. A third potential source for new ideas is to examine the seasons. Ask your company: "What product or service do we have that reflects the buying seasons (Christmas, Valentine's Day, Easter, summer, school and fall, Halloween, and Thanksgiving)?"

Finally, listen to your customers. Many times this source of new ideas is overlooked. Ask people who use your products or services how they would change or improve your offerings.

Before deciding which new products or services to offer, criteria must be established which details which new idea will be adopted. Each idea for a new product or service should be questioned prior to adoption. The degree of compatibility with company objectives must be examined. How large is the market for this product or service? Who are the competitors in this market? Are the resources (skill, time, money, personnel) available to make this product? As each idea goes through this screening, its potential to the company will surface. Exercise 2 and *Handout B*, as well as *Transparency 7*, will give participants some idea of the process that is undertaken when developing ideas for new products and services.

9 and 10. Target Markets

The identification and selection of target markets is a critical decision for companies. A target market is a relatively homogeneous group of people or organizations that have relatively similar product/service preferences with whom the company wishes to make an exchange. Once target markets have been identified, everything the company does must be tailored to the wants of this group. The process for breaking down the market place into small groups is known as market segmentation.

Several variables are used to segment markets. These variables, described earlier in "Knowing Your Customer," are used to break markets down into more manageable units. This process recognizes that different customer groups have different wants, which may justify the development of new products or services for the selected target market. Participants will get some practice in defining target markets in Exercise 2 and *Handout B*. *Transparency 8* also defines the target market.

11. The Product Life Cycle

Products and services go through changes over time. This process is called the Product Life Cycle (PLC). The four stages which comprise the PLC are: Introduction, Growth, Maturity and Decline.

In the *Introduction* stage, the product is introduced to the marketplace. For the first time, customers will hear about the product or service.

The *Growth* stage is characterized by rapid growth, high sales and high demand for the product or service.

In the *Maturity* stage, sales level off. Companies can decide to modify the product ("new and enhanced"), or they may terminate, or retrench, the product or service.

During the *Decline* stage, most products are terminated, because sales have fallen dramatically.

Some discussion of the PLC should be facilitated when participants have completed Exercise 3. The stages are also outlined on *Transparency 10*.

12. Retrenchment

The life cycle concept suggests that no product or service will deliver huge returns forever. Termination of the product or service is necessary.

All products and services become obsolete. These procedures for termination are necessary.

1. Collect data on the costs and benefits of the product or service. Find out how much it costs to deliver the specific product or service and what the sales of the item are. Product life cycles for products and services provide a great deal of information for termination.
2. The next stage in the process is to evaluate all products or services identified for retrenchment. Use agreed-upon criteria to rank the products. Ask what would happen if you withdraw the product or service.

Retrenchment can be accomplished by sudden withdrawal of the product, gradual withdrawal, or reduction in resources.

Finally, companies must implement the retrenchment process. Participants will get some idea of this process when doing Exercise 3 and *Handout C. Transparency 9* lists the steps of product retrenchment in a visual-aid format.

13 and 14. Communication and Promotion

Companies communicate with customers using a range of promotional techniques. Five promotional techniques are: personal selling, advertising, publicity and public relations, sales promotion and word of mouth.

Personal selling refers to face-to-face contact designed to persuade a customer to purchase a service or product.

Publicity refers to coverage of a service or product in the news media. *Sales promotions* create exposure for the product or service through incentive or discount programs. Incentives are used to persuade customers to try a product or service.

Word of mouth occurs when customers talk about products and services. Word of mouth is crucial to the success of most products and services. Positive word of mouth communication will stimulate sales, whereas negative word of mouth will contribute to a decline in sales. This information is made practical when participants complete Exercise 4. *Transparencies 11* and *12* list some types of product promotion and communication. Also, participants should be given *Handout D.*

15. Basic Elements of Service Quality

Service quality refers to delivering the promised product or service to the customer. Customers often use five general dimensions to judge service quality. They are reliability, tangibles, responsiveness, assurance and empathy.

Reliability refers to the ability to perform the promised services dependably and accurately. Tangibles describe the appearance of staff, equipment, resources and communication materials. Responsiveness is the willingness to help customers and to provide prompt service. Assurance is described as the knowledge and courtesy of employees. Finally, empathy refers to the provision of caring, individualized attention to the customers. Exercise 5 and *Handout E* are to be used with this section, as well as with the next section, "Procedures for Handling Customer Complaints."

16. Procedures for Handling Customer Complaints

Many times companies do not deliver the service right the first time. As a result, customers complain.

Companies should recognize that customers will have problems with products and services. Let your customers tell their story. Be sure to acknowledge that their point is important. The next step in the process is to find out what happened. Once the problem has been identified, decide what you can do to resolve the problem.

It is important to remember that most customers with complaints have truly experienced a problem. Use *Transparency 13*, *Handout E* and Exercise 5 to give participants some ideas for handling customer complaints.

Upon completion of the Marketing chapter, use *Transparency 14* to summarize the key points of the session.

Marketing

Exercises, Handouts and Transparencies

Exercise 1: Focus on Your Company (Instructor Notes)

Have each participant complete *Handout A* individually, then divide them into small groups. Instruct the group members to share their individual answers with the group, and then combine everyone's answers together. Each group should select a spokesperson, who will report their answers to the rest of the participants.

The instructor should point out that every company should know what their particular "business" is, and that each should operate using a "marketing orientation."

HANDOUT A

Focus on Your Company

1. Describe your company. Who are you?
2. What does your company offer (describe your products and/or services)?
3. Whom does your company serve (who are your customers)?
4. Where are you located?
5. If I was a customer of my company, I would want . . . (fill in the blank; Think of as many examples as possible.)

Exercise 2: Developing New Products and Services (Instructor Notes)

Participants should be divided into small groups for this exercise. They may either remain in the same groups that they formed for Exercise 1, or the instructor may wish for them to form new ones. Distribute a copy of *Handout B* to each person, but allow the group members to discuss the questions. Group brainstorming is a good technique to help participants think of as many answers as possible. Circulate throughout the room and offer assistance or a "jump-start" to those groups who need a little help. After each group has completed the exercise, they should select a new spokesperson, who will relay their answers to the entire group. A discussion should be centered around each group's answers and ideas before the next group presents their answers.

Exercise 3: Retrenchment (Instructor Notes)

Participants can remain in the small groups that they worked in for Exercise 2. Distribute a copy of *Handout C* to each participant, and have them discuss the questions with the group, as well as complete the handouts individually. After each group is finished, have them select a new spokesperson. The spokesperson should present the group's ideas with the entire group. After each individual group's presentation, the rest of the participants can discuss and give suggestions to the presenting group. The instructor should tie information about the Product Life Cycle (PLC) into this discussion. The instructor should also lead the discussion into which type of termination strategy the company should use when withdrawing its product from the market.

Exercise 4: Communications and Promotion (Instructor Notes)

The same small groups can complete this activity. Each group member should be given a copy of *Handout D*. Upon jointly completing the hand-

HANDOUT B

Developing New Products and Services
1. List your company's products and the benefits that they offer consumers.

Products   Benefits
2. List the target market for each product or service you offer.

Product/Service   Target market
3. List three (3) new products or services that your company will develop within the next 12 months, as well as its expected benefits and target market.

Product 1   **Date**

Purpose
Benefit
Target market

Product 2   **Date**

Purpose
Benefit
Target market

Product 3   **Date**

Purpose
Benefit
Target market

HANDOUT C

Retrenchment

1. Identify a product or service that your company will be withdrawing from the marketplace within the next 12 months.

2. List below the reasons for withdrawing this particular product or service from the marketplace.

3. List below the steps that your company might take in withdrawing the product.

out, the group should select a new spokesperson. After each group makes it's presentation, the instructor should encourage a large group discussion about the advantages and disadvantages of each communication method and theme.

HANDOUT D

Communications and Promotion

1. List five (5) methods of communication that your company will use to communicate with potential customers within the next 12 months, for two of your products or services.

Product/Service 1

1.
2.
3.
4.
5.

Product/Service 2

1.
2.
3.
4.
5.

2. List the month of the year that you will begin each communication method listed above (list the dates beside each method).

3. For one of your company's products or services, develop a new communication theme or message.

Product name:

Theme/message:

4. Describe how this new theme or message can communicate to potential customers the benefits of your product or service.

Exercise 5: Service Quality (Instructor Notes)

Again, the participants may remain in the same small groups that they formed for previous exercises. Each participant should complete a copy of *Handout E*, but they may discuss the questions in their groups. A new spokesperson should be selected, and the group's answers should be shared with the rest of the participants. The discussion should be centered around the concepts of service quality and complaint handling, as well as their relationships to word-of-mouth communication.

HANDOUT E

Service Quality

1. List 5 key words which describe your company's approach to service.

1.
2.
3.
4.
5.

2. Describe how your company will handle customer complaints.

3. For one (1) product or service, explain how you will deliver quality service.

Transparency 1

Marketing is a set of activities
aimed at facilitating
and expediting exchanges.

Transparency 2

Marketing Orientation
Visitor Wants

Promotional	Programs/
Effort	Attractions
	Mix

Transparency 3

Exchange

Delivers Products/Services that Provide Benefits

Company   Markets

Support, Dollars, Time

Transparency 4

The Marketing
Mix

- Product/Service
- Price
- Promotion
- Place

Transparency 5

Services vs. Products

- Intangibility
- Homogeneity
- Perishability
- Inseparability

Transparency 6

Know Your Customers

Who-   Total number
            Characteristics
            Market segment
            Party size
            Repeat visitors

Where-   Zip codes

How-   How do they plan their
            purchases?
            How far in advance?
            Who decides?

Why-   Purpose
            Benefits

Transparency 7

Developing New Products/Services

- Look into the future
- Look at the environment
- Look at the seasons
- Listen to customers

Transparency 8

Target Markets

Target market: A relatively homogeneous group of people that have relatively similar customer preferences with whom you wish to exchange.

Transparency 9

Retrenchment Procedures

• Identify the product or service to be terminated
• Evaluate
• Select termination strategy
• Implement

Transparency 10

The Product Life Cycle

There are four stages in the PLC:

• <u>Introduction</u> of product to the marketplace
• <u>Growth</u> (high demand and high sales)
• <u>Maturity</u> (sales level off)
• <u>Decline</u> (product is terminated)

Transparency 11

Five Types of Promotion

• Personal selling
• Advertising
• Publicity/Public relations
• Sales promotion
• Word of mouth

Transparency 12

Communication Techniques
Ex. Advertising

• Newspapers
• Direct mail
• Television
• Magazines
• Radio
• Outdoor advertising
• Brochure distribution

Transparency 13

Handling Customer Complaints

- Recognize and deal with customers as people.
- Let the customer tell his story—don't interrupt.
- Acknowledge that their point is important.
- Express sincere concern.
- Find out exactly what has upset the customer.
- Offer a solution—get agreement that the solution will solve the problem.
- End with an apology and invite the customer to do business with you again.
- Contact the customer one week later to assure his satisfaction.

Transparency 14

Marketing
Key Points

1. Marketing is the set of activities aimed at facilitating and expediting an exchange.

2. When a company offers a product or service to a customer, and the customer values and purchases this product or service, an exchange has been made.

3. The "Four Ps" of marketing:

   - Product
   - Place
   - Price
   - Promotion

4. A target market is the group of customers with whom a company wishes to make an exchange.

5. Retrenchment is the process of withdrawing a product from the market.

6. Most customers who have a complaint have truly experienced a problem with your product or service.

References

Akeret, R.V. (1991). *Family tales, family wisdom: How to gather the stories of a lifetime and share these with your family.* New York: William Morrow and Company, Inc.

Alder & Towne. (1996). *Looking out/looking in* (8th ed.). Fort Worth, TX: Holt, Rinehart and Winston.

Antonucci, T.C. (1990). Social supports and social relationships. In R.H. Binstock and L.K. George (Eds.), *Handbook of aging and social sciences*, 3rd ed. (pp. 205-227). San Diego: Academic Press.

Banks, J. & Banks, C. (1993). *Multicultural issues and perspectives* (2nd ed.). Needman Heights, MA: Allyn and Bacon.

Beale, G.M., Bohlen, J.M., & Raudabaugh, J.W. (1962). *Leadership and dynamic group action.* Ames, IA: Iowa State University Press.

Bengtson, V. L., Schaie, K., & Burton, L.M. (1995). *Adult Intergenerational Relations: Effects of Societal Change.* New York, NY: Springer Publishing Company.

Biaga, B. (1978). *Working together: A manual for helping groups work more effectively.* Amherst, MA: University of Massachusetts, Citizen Involvement Training Project Books, Inc.

Business Partnerships Work Force Programs Department (1993). *How to recruit older workers.* Washington, DC: American Association of Retired Persons.

Cartwright, D. & Zander, A. (1960). *Group dynamics: Research and theory.* New York: Harper & Row.

Chapman, N.J., & Neal, M.B. (1990). The effect of intergenerational experiences on adolescents and older adults. *The Gerontologist, 30*(6), 825-832.

Cherry, D.L., Benest, F.R., Gates, B., & White, J. (1985). Intergenerational service programs: Meeting shared needs of young and old. *The Gerontologist, 25*(2), 126-129.

Chronbach, L.J. (1982). Prudent aspirations for social inquiry. In: W.H. Kruskal (Ed.), *The social sciences: Their nature and uses* (pp. 61-81). Chicago: University of Chicago Press.

Cleinbell, H.J. (1972). *The people dynamic: Changing self and society through growth groups.* New York: Harper & Row.

Cook, Fay L. (1992). Ageism: Rhetoric and reality. *The Gerontologist, 32*(3), 292-293.

Davis, S. & Ferdman, B. (1993). *Nourishing the heart.* New York: New York Center for Urban Folk Culture.

DeBoard, K.B. & Flanagan, V. (1994). Bridging the gap: Intergenerational programs. (INTERNET REF).

Dryfoos, J.G. (1990). *Adolescents at risk: Prevalence and prevention.* New York: Oxford University Press.

Dyer, W.G. (1972). *Modern theory and method in group training.* New York: Von Nostrand Reinhold.

Ellis, S. (1994). *The volunteer recruitment book.* Philadelphia, PA: Energize, Inc.

Elmore, D. (1996). Retirement community develops on-site preschool. KINnections Magazine. Available at http://www.ott.net/kin/kinmag.htm.

Fisher, J. & Cole, K. (1993). *Leadership and management of volunteer programs: A guide for volunteer administrators.* San Francisco, CA: Jossey-Bass.

Fisher, L. R. & Schaffer, K.B. (1993). *Older volunteers: A guide to research and practice.* Newbury Park: Sage Publications.

Fisher, R. & Ury, W. (1981). *Getting to yes: Negotiating agreement without giving in.* Boston, MA: Houghton-Mifflin Co.

Freedman, M. (1988). *Partners in growth: Elder mentors and at-risk youth.* Philadelphia: Public/Private Ventures.

Friedman, B. (1996). The future is intergenerational: Let's begin. In Cram, M. & VanDerveer, B. (eds.), *Proceedings from the 1995 NRPA Regional and National Intergenerational Institute*, pp. 113-128.

Funk, P. (1996). It pays to enrich your word power. *Reader's Digest. 149*(893), 171-172.

Fuoss, D.E., & Troppmann, R.J. (1981). *Effective coaching: A psychological approach.* New York: John Wiley & Sons.

Garfield, O. (1971). *Parliamentary procedure at a glance.* Binghamton: Hawthorn.

Garrison, M., & Bly, M.A. (1997). *Human relations: Productive approaches for the workplace.* Needham Heights, MA: Allyn & Bacon.

Halberg, K. (1995). *If you don't evaluate, it didn't happen: Evaluating intergenerational programs.* In proceedings from 1995 NRPA Intergenerational Institutes, San Antonio, TX.

Harel, Z., McKinney, E., & Williams, M. (1990). *Black Aged: Understanding Diversity and Service Needs.* Newbury Park, CA: Sage Publications.

Haskett, B., & Ogilivie, J.R. (1996). Feedback processes in task groups. In Cathcart, Samovar, and Henman, *Small group communication theory and practice* (7th ed., pp. 254-267). Dubuque, IA: Brown & Benchmark.

Henderson, K.A. (1995). *Evaluation leisure services: Making enlightened decisions.* State College, PA: Venture Publishing.

Herman, J.L., Lyons-Morris, L. & Fritz-Gibbon, C.T. C. (1987). *Evaluator's handbook.* Newbury Park, CA: Sage Publications.

Holmes, E.R. & Holmes, L.D. (1995). *Other Cultures, Elder Years.* Thousand Oaks, CA: Sage Publications.

Intergenerational projects idea book. (1993). Washington, DC: American Association of Retired People.

Jackson, Linda A. & Sullivan, L. (1987). Age stereotype disconfirming information and evaluations of old people. *The Journal of Social Psychology. 128*(6), 721-729.

Jacobs, A., & Spradlin, W.W. (1974). *The group as agent of change.* New York: Behavioral Publications.

Jessor, R. (1992). Risk behavior in adolescence: A psychosocial framework for understanding and action. In D.E. Rogers & E. Ginsburg (Eds.), *Adolescents at risk: Medical and social perspectives.* Boulder, CO: Westview Press.

Jessor, R., Van Den Bos, J., Vanderryn, J., Costa, F.M., & Turbin, M. (1994). *Protective factors in adolescent problem behavior: Moderator effects and developmental change.* Manuscript submitted for publication.

Jessor, R., Van Den Bos, J., Vanderryn, J., Costa, F.M., & Turbin, M. (1994). Protective factors in adolescent problem behavior: Moderator effects and developmental change. *Journal of Developmental Psychology.* Under review (pp. 4-5).

Johnson, A., Pentz, M.A., Weber, M.D., Dwyer, J., Baer, N., Mackinnon, Hansen, W.B., & Flay, B.R. (1990). Relative effectiveness of comprehensive community programming for drug abuse prevention with high-risk and low-risk adolescents. *Journal of Consulting and Clinical Psychology. 58*(4), 447-456.

Johnson, D.W., & Johnson, F.P. (1982). *Joining together: Group theory and group skills.* Englewood Cliffs, NJ: Prentice-Hall.

Jordan, D.J. (1996). *Leadership in leisure services: Making a difference.* State College, PA: Venture Publishing Inc.

Kaplan, M. (1994). *Side by side: Exploring your neighborhood through intergenerational activities.* Berkeley: MIG Communications.

Keith, J., Fry, C.L., Glascock, A.P., Ikels, C., Dickerson-Putman, J., Harpending, H.C., & Draper, P. (1994). *The Aging Experience: Diversity and Commonality Across Cultures.* Thousand Oaks, CA: Sage Publications.

Kin Intergenerational Excellence Awards (1996). Phone pals. Available at http:/ott.net/~kin/xawards.htm

Knowles, M. (1959). *Introduction to group dynamics.* New York: Association Press.

Kraus, R., Carpenter, G., & Bates, B. (1981). *Recreation leadership and supervision: Guidelines for professional development* (2nd ed.). Philadelphia: Saunders College Publishing.

Krout, J. (1993). *Senior Center Evaluation: A technical assistance guide for providers of services to the aging.* Washington, DC: National Council on the Aging, Inc.

Larke, P.J. (1991). Multicultural education: A vital investment strategy for cultural diverse youths groups. *Journal of the Southeastern Association of Educational Opportunities for Program Personnel, 10,*11-22.

Leadership in Groups and Organizations (1984). Community Resource Development, Virginia Cooperative Extension Service Correspondence Course.

Leigololu, A. (1996). Available at http://wwweds.tamu.edu/alhtdocs/inter gen.html.

Locke, D.C. (1992). *Increasing Multicultural Understanding: A Comprehensive Model.* Newbury Park, CA: Sage Publications.

Luft, J. (1970). *An introduction to group dynamics* (2nd ed.). Palo Alto, CA: National Press Books.

Lussier, R.N. (1996). *Human Relations in Organizations: A skill-building approach* (3rd ed.). Chicago: Richard D. Irwin.

Lutz, S. & Haller, J. (1996). *Seniors and children: Building bridges together.* Washington, DC: The National Council on Aging.

McAdoo, H.P. (1993). *Family Ethnicity: Strength in Diversity.* Newbury Park, CA: Sage Publications.

McCurley, S. & Vineyard, S. (1988). *101 tips for volunteer recruitment.* Downers Grove, IL: Heritage Arts.

Mead, M. (1978). *Culture and commitment.* New York, NY: Columbia University Press.

Mead, M. (1974). Grandparents as Educators. In H. J. Leichter (Ed.), *The family as educator.* New York: Teachers College Press.

Milliken, W.E. (1994). Youths at risk and dropout prevention: A working program. In B. Cato, H. Gray, D. Nelson, and P.R. Vames (Eds.), *Youths at risk: Targeting in on prevention* (pp. 57-60). Dubuque, IA: William C. Brown Communications, Inc.

Mills, J. (1983). Multicultural education: Where do we go from here? *Journal of Social and Behavioral Sciences, 9,*45-51.

Napier, R.W., & Gershenfield, N.Y. (1973). *Groups: Theory and experience.* Boston, MA: Houghton Mifflin Co.

Newman, S. (1989). A history of intergenerational programs. *Journal of Children in Contemporary Society, 20*(3/4), 1-16.

Palmore, Erdman B. (1988). *The facts on aging quiz.* New York: Springer Publishing Company.

Patton, M.Q. (1990). *Qualitative Evaluation and Research Methods* (2nd ed.). Newbury Park, CA: Sage Publications.

Powell, J. & Arquitt, G.E. (1978). Getting the generations back together: A rationale for the development of community-based intergenerational interaction programs. *The Family Coordinator, 28*(4), 421-426.

Rich, P.E., Myrick, R.D., & Campbell, C. (1983). Changing children's perceptions of the elderly. *Educational Gerontology, 9,*483-491.

Rossi, P.H. & Freeman, H.E. (1993). *Evaluation: A systematic approach* (5th ed.). Newbury Park, CA: Sage Publication.

Scannell, T. & Roberts, A. (1994). *Young and old serving together: Meeting community needs through intergenerational partnerships.* Washington, DC: Generations United.

Schiman, C. and Lordeman, A. (1989, December). *A study of the use of volunteers by long term care ombudsman programs: The effectiveness of recruitment, supervision and retention.* Washington, DC: The National Association of State Units on Aging, The National Center for State Long Term Care Ombudsman Resources.

Sessoms, H.D. & Stevenson, J.L. (1981). *Leadership and group dynamics in recreation services.* Reading, MA: Addison-Wesley Publishing Co.

Shaw, M.E. (1976). *Group dynamics: The psychology of small group behavior.* New York: McGraw-Hill.

Sleeter, C.E. (1991). *Empowerment through multicultural education.* Albany, NY: State University of New York Press.

Smink, J. & Stank, P.C. (1992). *The evaluation handbook: Guidelines for evaluating dropout prevention programs.* Clemson, SC: National Dropout Prevention Center.

Steinberg, L.R. (1996). *Adolescence.* New York, NY: McGraw-Hill, Inc.

Stoller, E.P. & Gibson, R.C. (1994). *Worlds of Difference: Inequality in the Aging Experience.* Thousand Oaks, CA: Pine Forge Press.

Strasburger, V. (1993). *Getting your kids to say no in the 90s when you said yes in the 60s.* New York, NY: Simon & Schuster.

Sum, A.M. & Fogg, W.N. (1991). The adolescent poor and the transition to early adulthood. In P.B. Edelman & J. Ladner (Eds.), *Adolescence and poverty: Challenge for the 1990s.* Washington, DC: Center for National Policy Press.

Teenagers + senior citizens = crime-busting combination. (1992, Winter). *Profiles.*

Tubbs, S.L. (1978). *A systems approach to small group interaction.* Reading, MA: Addison-Wesley Publishing Co.

The two of us: A handbook for mentors. (pp. 6-16). Baltimore, MD: The Abell Foundation.

Vineyard, S. (1984, Spring). Recruiting and retaining volunteers: No gimmicks, no gags! *The Journal of Volunteer Administration, 2*(3)*,* 23-28.

Wynn, M. (1992). *Empowering African American males to succeed: A ten step approach for parents and teachers.* Marietta , GA: The Rising Sun Publishing.

Youth and elderly team up for program fighting crime. (1990, October 1). *The Florida Times Union.*

Resource List

The Abell Foundation
1116 Fidelity Building
210 N. Charles St.
Baltimore, MD 21201
(410)685-8316

American Association of Retired Persons–AARP
601 E Street, N.W.
Washington, DC 20049

Family Tales. Family Wisdom: How to Gather the Stories
of a Lifetime and Share These with Your Family,
by Dr. Robert V. Akeret (with Daniel Klein)

Family Tales. Family Wisdom outlines successful ways of weaving together the stories of a life-time–stories which help us to make sense of our lives. In his book, Dr. Akeret provides detailed approaches to organizing stories around personal themes by setting up different storytelling sessions (e.g., Snapshots From Your Youth, A Day in Your Life, and Epiphanies and Lessons). It also provides a wide range of information on how to make optimum use of memory triggers such as old photos, letters, passports, ticket stubs and other "treasures in the bottom of the drawer."

Family Tales, Family Wisdom (1991) is published by William Morrow and Company, Inc., 1358 Avenue of the Americas, New York, NY 10019 ($17.00).

Group Dynamics: Research and Theory, by Dorwin Cartwright

The nature of group cohesiveness is outlined in *Group Dynamics,* along with the pressures of accomplishing uniformity in groups. The book also discusses power, influence, leadership and performance in groups and group functions. Lastly, *Group Dynamics* explains motivational and structural properties in groups.

Group Processes: An Introduction to Group Dynamics, by Joseph Luft

Group Processes introduces the idea of group dynamics. It further explains ways of studying group processes and the role of the teacher in group dynamics. Along with these basic explanations of group dynamics, the book explains *The Johari Window*, a graphic model of awareness in interpersonal relations.

The Histop Manual, edited by Nancy Rosen, 1983

HISTOP is an acronym for History Sharing Through Our Photographs. It is a program created in 1979 to promote the sharing of history through family photographs, and to teach both old and young the importance of photographs as historical documents. HISTOP involves its participants in activities that stimulate creativity, impart useful knowledge and afford opportunities for intergenerational communication. It is designed to be as flexible as possible regarding group size and scheduling, and can be implemented at minimal cost.

The manual also provides suggestions for developing partnerships with museums in your community. It is available from *Lynda Ianni, Michigan Humanities Council, 19 Pere Marquette Drive, #3B, Lansing, MI 48912-1231.*

Introduction to Group Dynamics, by Malcolm Shepherd Knowles

Introduction to Group Dynamics gives the reader a historical perspective in group dynamics. It also provides an understanding for individual and group behavior. Finally, *Introduction to Group Dynamics* provides practical applications in dealing with group dynamics.

Know Your Customer: New Approaches to Understanding Customer Value and Satisfaction, by Robert B. Woodruff

Know Your Customer focuses on the new perspective of customer value and links it to customer satisfaction. The book also describes the importance of coming to know your customer through the methods customer value determination and predicting customer value.

Leadership and Group Dynamics in Recreation Services,
by H. Douglas Sessoms and Jack Lovett Stevenson

Leadership and Group Dynamics in Recreation Services examines the theories of leadership, while looking at the recreator involved in group dynamics. The book looks at the recreation system and both small and large group techniques. The book also provides many group problems for the reader to consider.

Learning from the Past, by Bi-Folkal Productions

Bi-Folkal Productions, Inc. recently published *Learning from the Past*, a guide to using their multi-media, multi-sensory program kits in schools and intergenerational settings. The introduction to the guide includes rationale, teaching strategy, preparation (instructional design and practical planning), learning experiences (establishing a sense of time), and resources. The guide is printed on loose-leaf pages and packages in a sturdy three-ring binder. *Learning from the Past* will be invaluable to teachers, librarians, scout leaders, and anyone else ready to build a bridge between people of two generations.

Bi-Folkal Productions, Inc. is a non-profit corporation, organized to encourage creative programming with older adults and the sharing of experiences between the generations. To order or obtain further information, call Bi-Folkal Productions, Inc. at 608/251-2818 or fax 608/251-2874.

Managing Customer Value: Creating Quality and Service that Customers Can See, by Bradley T. Gale

Managing Customer Value explains how to make quality a strategic weapon. The book also discusses who the role models are and how to manage big issues with the idea of customer value management. Finally, *Managing Customer Value* describes the pay offs of super quality.

The National Dropout Prevention Center
205 Martin Street
Clemson, SC 29634
(803)656-2599

Nourishing the Heart, by Shari Davis and Benny Ferdman, 1993

Nourishing the Heart, a new guide to intergenerational arts projects in schools, has just been published. The title makes reference to the metaphor of cooking its authors Shari Davis and Benny Ferdman use throughout the book. The authors contend that in bringing up children today, one essential ingredient is often missing–an older person whose wisdom and influence enriches and adds flavor and spice to the experience of growing up. The authors provide clear instructions for setting up and sustaining school-based programs that include this important ingredient.

The book distills the best ideas of dozens of artists who worked within New York's Arts Partners Program. These artists implemented a number of imaginative projects that explored diverse themes and resulted in strikingly different works of art, from puppet shows which explore community history to a picnic table laden with crafted objects symbolizing family outings.

Nourishing the Heart is available without charge for teachers, and for $10 for others. All orders must include $12 for postage and handling. Contact City Lore: The New York Center for Urban Folk Culture, 72 East First Street, New York, NY 10003, (212)529-1953.

South Carolina Human Affairs Commission

The South Carolina Human Affairs Commission runs "communication training" sessions which deal with a number of diversity topics.

Contact Mary Sneed at P.O. Box 4490, Columbia, SC 29240, or call (803)253-6336.

Study Circles Resource Center

This organization publishes manuals which outline how to run nonconfrontational "study circles" pertaining to several topics; race relations is just one of them. For information, contact them at P.O. Box 203, Pomfret, CT 06258, or call (203) 928-2616.

WEBSITES

http://www.aoa.dhhs.gov/aoa/webres/org.htm
Directory of WEB and Gopher Sites on Aging developed by Administration on Aging, U.S. Dept. of Health and Human Services.
http://www.careerspot.com/vitalsigns/sc3vs32.htm
The Older Adult Services Department at Lee Memorial Hospital in Fort Myers, FL offers a program to help build sensitivity to aging.

http://www.inservice.com/index.html
> "In Service Works" offers a video series which explores and teaches respect for the diversity found in today's classrooms.

http://tel.occe.uoknor.edu/swrc/culpos.html
> A cultural sensitivity position paper by the Southwest Regional Center for drug-free schools and communities.

http://www.strom.clemson.edu/teams/risl/
> Retirement and Intergenerational Studies Laboratory at the Strom Thurmond Institute, Clemson University.

http://www.temple.edu/departments/CIL/
> Temple University Center for Intergenerational Learning.

http://www3.pitt.edu/~gti/
> Generations Together: An Intergenerational Studies Program.

Group Dynamics–http://www.abacon.com/list/se0114.html
Small Group Dynamics–http://smallgroups.com/dynamics.htm
Team Building–http://www.teamtechnology.co.uk/tt/h-articl/tb-basic.htm

Center for Intergenerational Learning (1996a). New Initiatives at CIL. Interchange, Spring, 1996. Available at:
http://www.temple.edu/departments/CIL/interchange.html.

Center for Intergenerational Learning (1996b). Spotlight #2: The time out program. Interchange, Spring, 1996. Available at:
http://www.temple.edu/departments/CIL/interchange.

Index

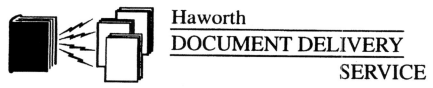

Haworth
DOCUMENT DELIVERY
SERVICE

This valuable service provides a single-article order form for any article from a Haworth journal.

- *Time Saving:* No running around from library to library to find a specific article.
- *Cost Effective:* All costs are kept down to a minimum.
- *Fast Delivery:* Choose from several options, including same-day FAX.
- *No Copyright Hassles:* You will be supplied by the original publisher.
- *Easy Payment:* Choose from several easy payment methods.

Open Accounts Welcome for ...
- Library Interlibrary Loan Departments
- Library Network/Consortia Wishing to Provide Single-Article Services
- Indexing/Abstracting Services with Single Article Provision Services
- Document Provision Brokers and Freelance Information Service Providers

---

MAIL or *FAX* THIS ENTIRE ORDER FORM TO:

Haworth Document Delivery Service
The Haworth Press, Inc.
10 Alice Street
Binghamton, NY 13904-1580

or **FAX:** 1-800-895-0582
or **CALL:** 1-800-342-9678
9am-5pm EST

PLEASE SEND ME PHOTOCOPIES OF THE FOLLOWING SINGLE ARTICLES:
1) Journal Title: _____
   Vol/Issue/Year: _____ Starting & Ending Pages: _____
   Article Title: _____
   _____

2) Journal Title: _____
   Vol/Issue/Year: _____ Starting & Ending Pages: _____
   Article Title: _____
   _____

3) Journal Title: _____
   Vol/Issue/Year: _____ Starting & Ending Pages: _____
   Article Title: _____
   _____

4) Journal Title: _____
   Vol/Issue/Year: _____ Starting & Ending Pages: _____
   Article Title: _____
   _____

(See other side for Costs and Payment Information)

COSTS: Please figure your cost to order quality copies of an article.

1. Set-up charge per article: $8.00
   ($8.00 × number of separate articles) _____

2. Photocopying charge for each article:

   1-10 pages: $1.00 _____

   11-19 pages: $3.00 _____

   20-29 pages: $5.00 _____

   30+ pages: $2.00/10 pages _____

3. Flexicover (optional): $2.00/article _____

4. Postage & Handling: US: $1.00 for the first article/
   $.50 each additional article _____

   Federal Express: $25.00 _____

   Outside US: $2.00 for first article/
   $.50 each additional article _____

5. Same-day FAX service: $.35 per page _____

   GRAND TOTAL: _____

METHOD OF PAYMENT: (please check one)

❑ Check enclosed ❑ Please ship and bill. PO # _____
(sorry we can ship and bill to bookstores only! All others must pre-pay)

❑ Charge to my credit card: ❑ Visa; ❑ MasterCard; ❑ Discover;
   ❑ American Express;

Account Number: _____ Expiration date: _____

Signature: *X* _____

Name: _____ Institution: _____

Address: _____

_____

City: _____ State: _____ Zip: _____

Phone Number: _____ FAX Number: _____

MAIL or *FAX* THIS ENTIRE ORDER FORM TO:

Haworth Document Delivery Service
The Haworth Press, Inc.
10 Alice Street
Binghamton, NY 13904-1580

or FAX: 1-800-895-0582
or CALL: 1-800-342-9678
9am-5pm EST)